Do No Harm

DO NO HARM

HOW AID CAN SUPPORT
PEACE—OR WAR

Mary B. Anderson

LYNNE
RIENNER
PUBLISHERS

BOULDER
LONDON

Published in the United States of America in 1999 by
Lynne Rienner Publishers, Inc.
1800 30th Street, Boulder, Colorado 80301

and in the United Kingdom by
Lynne Rienner Publishers, Inc.
3 Henrietta Street, Covent Garden, London WC2E 8LU

Library of Congress Cataloging-in-Publication Data
Anderson, Mary B., 1939–
   Do no harm : how aid can support peace—or war / by Mary B.
Anderson.
      p.   cm.
   Includes bibliographical references and index.
   ISBN 1-55587-833-4 (alk. paper). — ISBN 1-55587-834-2 (pbk. :
alk. paper)
   1. Humanitarian assistance.   2. International relief.   3. War and
society.   I. Title.
HV544.5.A53   1999
361.2'6—dc21   98-44669
                                                                                     CIP

British Cataloguing in Publication Data
A Cataloguing in Publication record for this book
is available from the British Library.

Printed and bound in the United States of America

The paper used in this publication meets the requirements
of the American National Standard for Permanence of
Paper for Printed Library Materials Z39.48-1984.

5   4

Contents

v

103047

Part 3
Conclusion

Preface

I am often accused of a "rosy optimism" that seems to some to be naive and simplistic in light of recent war experiences. The fact is, I am optimistic because—even in the midst of the most demoralizing and degrading violence that humans seem capable of inflicting on each other—I have often met generosity, sacrifice, courage, and faith in human nature. These qualities continue to shape the ideas and behaviors of many people who, given their experiences, should have succumbed to selfishness, hatred, fear, and meanness.

In a very real sense, this book has been written by such people. Some are staff members of international and local nongovernmental organizations (NGOs) that provide humanitarian and development assistance in conflict zones. Others are the so-called victims of wars, people who live in societies that have fallen into intergroup warfare in the post–Cold War period.

The book reflects the insights gleaned from many people's experiences in providing and receiving aid in conflict areas, insights gathered through the Local Capacities for Peace Project. The project, run by the Collaborative for Development Action, Inc., is a joint effort of many NGOs, international donor agencies, agencies of the United Nations, and others involved in international assistance policies and programs. As director of the project, it is my privilege to write this book on behalf of all those who have collaborated on it. The book's focus is on using past experience to learn how to provide aid more effectively in the future. This purpose has united the rather disparate crowd that has been involved in collecting information, reflecting on it and debating its meaning, proposing interpretations of events, challenging those interpretations, and, in general, trying to learn what is to be learned about aid and conflict.

We have not all agreed on everything in the book. It is my advantage—and risk—finally to summarize what I believe our collective effort has produced so far. When the ideas and approaches ring "true" for the reader, everyone involved in the effort should be credited. If we later discover new ways of thinking that call into question some of the ideas presented here (or even prove them dead wrong), all of us will be pleased. We have not been and still are not doctrinaire in our presentation of the contents. The approach of the project continues to be exploratory, inquiring, and based on the personal experiences of people providing aid in the field. As these experiences change and more reflection, discussion, and debate about them occur, we will surely learn more. So this book is offered from and to the international assistance community as a step in the constant process of learning how to do our jobs better.

*   *   *

So many people deserve thanks and appreciation that, were I to mention them all, the book would double in size. Thus I must name only the few who have been the most involved, and on whom I relied most in choosing the ideas and words included here.

First is the group of donor agencies that provided financial support for the case studies, the "feedback" workshops during which aid people in many war zones and at NGO headquarters examined their own experiences and those of others to discern lessons, and the management of the entire process. These include the Canadian International Development Agency, the Danish Ministry of Foreign Affairs, the Evangelische Kirke für Entwicklungshilfe E.V., the Finnish Red Cross, the Office of Foreign Disaster Assistance of the U.S. Agency for International Development, the Royal Ministry of Foreign Affairs of Norway, the Swedish International Development and Cooperation Agency, the Swedish Red Cross, and the United Nations High Commissioner for Refugees. In addition, more than fifty other UN agencies, donor governments, and NGOs provided both cash and in-kind support for the writing of case studies, the running of workshops, and involvement in consultations.

Two specific groups must be named for their important work. The first includes the individuals and agencies that contributed case studies to the initial phase of the project. The individuals are Joe Bock, Kenny Gluck, Kate Halversen, Greg Hansen, Helene Holm-Pedersen, Stephen Jackson, Tom Lent, Sue Lycke, Larry Minear, Lena Salin, and Willet Weeks. The agencies include Agence Internationale Contre la Faim, Catholic Relief Services, Danish Refugee Council, International Catholic Migration Committee, International Committee of the Red Cross, International Federation of Red Cross and Red Crescent Societies, International Rescue Committee, Jerusalem Link, Médicines Sans

Frontières (France), Norwegian Church Aid, Norwegian Refugee Council, Pakrac Reconstruction Project (Croatia), Redd Barna, Research and Training Institute (Karachi, Pakistan), Save the Children Federation, St. Xavier's Social Service Society (Ahmedabad, India), Trocaire, United Methodist Committee on Relief, United Nations High Commissioner for Refugees, and United Nations Volunteers.

The second group includes the people most involved in running and managing the extensive series of feedback workshops. Greg Hansen deserves special mention for managing the complicated processes of arranging twenty-four such events in a one-year period, as well as for his role in helping to facilitate them. Other facilitators and, when relevant, the agencies that supported their involvement include Inger Björk (Swedish Red Cross), Joe Bock (Catholic Relief Services), Bob Burke (World Vision/International), Sam Engelstadt, Laura Frost, Kenny Gluck, Wolfgang Heinrich (Association of the Churches' Development Services [AG KED]), Stephen Jackson, Wolfgang Jamann (World Vision/Canada), Mark Janz (World Vision/International), Pia Jertfelt (Swedish Red Cross), Jørgen Kristensen (Danish Red Cross), Janis Lindsteadt (Catholic Relief Services), Per Midteide (Norwegian Church Aid), and Willet Weeks.

Finally, a small group of loyal actors read the entire manuscript and gave invaluable suggestions for its improvement. They include Everett Mendelsohn, who read with his usual sensitive ear for tone as well as substance; Kenny Gluck, who brought his broad experience and nuanced understanding of political realities to the task; and Marshall Wallace, who provided excellent editorial and organizational advice, as well as clarification of content. Others named earlier as case writers and workshop facilitators also read individual sections and chapters and corrected errors, added substance and examples, corrected misunderstandings, and generally provided the kind of "test" of facts and interpretations few authors enjoy. I cannot thank these people enough.

So the reader is indebted to all of these named and unnamed individuals for the merits of the book. I, too, am indebted to them for their support, help, and colleagueship. Although some of them have been among those who challenge my tone of rosy optimism, it is their dedication to "doing no harm" and "getting it right" with international aid that is in part responsible for it. I honor and thank them.

Mary B. Anderson

I

Introduction

When international assistance is given in the context of a violent conflict, it becomes a part of that context and thus also of the conflict. Although aid agencies often seek to be neutral or nonpartisan toward the winners and losers of a war, the impact of their aid is not neutral regarding whether conflict worsens or abates. When given in conflict settings, aid can reinforce, exacerbate, and prolong the conflict; it can also help to reduce tensions and strengthen people's capacities to disengage from fighting and find peaceful options for solving problems. Often, an aid program does some of both: in some ways it worsens the conflict, and in others it supports disengagement. But in all cases aid given during conflict cannot remain separate from that conflict.

This is a book about how aid and conflict interact. Based on broad experience of providing international assistance in conflict settings, it is neither theoretical nor speculative. The data are facts gleaned from past action and what has been learned from that action.

The chapters that follow cite experiences and examples from numerous aid projects and programs around the world. These examples have been gathered through the Local Capacities for Peace Project, which is a collaborative effort involving international and local nongovernmental organizations (NGOs), UN agencies, and European and North American donor governments.

The purpose of the project is to answer the question, How can humanitarian or development assistance be given in conflict situations in ways that rather than feeding into and exacerbating the conflict help local people to disengage and establish alternative systems for dealing with the problems that underlie the conflict? The approach has been to collect case studies of aid experiences in conflict areas and to consult broadly, through a series of feedback workshops and other meetings, with numerous aid staff members and recipients in many local settings to gather past experiences and learn from them.[1] Numerous individuals and agencies have collaborated on the ideas reported in this book.

Early in our efforts to learn from broad and seemingly disparate experiences, we were overwhelmed by the differences encountered. Each war is unique; each society has its own history, culture, personages, values, and tensions. Every aid project site is local and special. Aid workers join local people in describing their setting in specific detail and in emphasizing its uniqueness and its oddities.

As the individual stories accumulated, however, common themes, repeated trends, and consistent patterns emerged. Although each place and each people is unique, each also shares commonalities with all others. The interactions of external aid with the internal, local workings of specific societies produce familiar, repeated outcomes. When such patterns emerge it is often possible to predict them, and with the ability to anticipate aid's impacts on conflict the possibility arises of avoiding the negative effects and enhancing the positive ones.

Many people criticize international assistance, accurately citing examples of ways in which international aid has done harm rather than good. We note such examples, but we do not condemn aid for its failures. It is a moral and logical fallacy to conclude that because aid can do harm, a decision *not* to give aid would do no harm. In reality, a decision to withhold aid from people in need would have unconscionable negative ramifications.

We believe international aid is a good thing. We think the world is a better place because when some people suffer, other people who are able to take actions to help lessen that suffering do so. The challenge we see for aid workers—and for the large number of generous and caring individuals who support their work with financial and material contributions—is to figure out how to do the good they mean to do without inadvertently undermining local strengths, promoting dependency, and allowing aid resources to be misused in the pursuit of war.

The premise of this book—again based on the experiences of many people in conflict zones around the world—is that aid agencies have a new and profound opportunity to shape their relief and development work so it accomplishes its intended goals of alleviating human suffering and supporting the pursuit of sustainable economic and social systems and at the same time promotes durable and just peace. The opportunity is new because the situations in which aid workers find themselves are often different today from those in even the very recent past. The opportunity is profound because in the face of these differences, the role for grassroots action in relation to high-level diplomatic efforts to resolve conflict is as great as ever in our history. Nongovernmental organizations—the primary operational arm of the large relief and development aid enterprise—are and can be positioned to support peace and negate war as never before. This premise will be explained and illustrated in each chapter of the book.

The premise does not imply that aid agencies should become peace agencies. In fact, we argue that relief and development assistance is so important and the skills required to be effective in providing aid are so specialized that aid agencies should remain true to their original mandates and continue to do what they know how to do best. But as the experience we cite shows, even as these agencies provide emergency and long-term aid, they have opportunities to do so in ways that support peace rather than war.

Our purpose is to improve aid. It is a practical purpose. In fact, we were first motivated to undertake this project when we heard many aid workers in many settings describe the difficulties they encountered in providing aid in conflict situations. They saw the ways their aid fed into conflict and sought ideas about how to avoid this. Thus in this book we have gathered experiences and identified common patterns to provide aid workers with a strong background of collective learning on which to make better choices and decisions so that aid will do no harm and instead will do the good we mean it to do.

The book is organized in three parts. Part 1 presents lessons learned from experience and illustrates how in some cases aid has done harm and in others has avoided doing harm and has instead been able to strengthen local capacities for peace in conflict areas. The last chapter in Part 1 brings these lessons together into an analytical framework that is offered as a practical planning and evaluation tool for aid workers.

Part 2 presents selected case studies of aid experiences in conflict areas that report lessons learned in specific places and times. These cases give only a taste of the raw data from which the ideas in this book arose. They are powerful testimony to the many people who have put themselves on the line to provide aid because it is needed and, at the same time, who have maintained an attitude of self-criticism and open inquiry regarding aid's impacts, holding themselves accountable for what they are doing. Part 3 includes a brief conclusion that points ahead to the areas where more work is needed. Although more (always!) remains to be learned, much has also been learned. If the lessons reported here were integrated into the daily actions of aid workers, the impacts of aid on conflict would support, encourage, and strengthen the capacities of people in conflict-ridden societies to end the fighting and find other ways to achieve the changes they seek.

PART ONE

---

*War and the Impact
of External Aid*

2

Today's Wars and the Pursuit of Justice

Throughout this book, we assert that international aid given in a conflict setting should not feed into and exacerbate the conflict. This position is often challenged. Many people feel conflict can be healthy. Avoidance of conflict for its own sake is wrong-minded, they claim, because people contend for important purposes. By failing to support people engaged in a battle for justice, we support the status quo of injustice. NGOs must be clearly on the side of those who are poor and marginalized, those against whom societies discriminate, and their aid must support systemic change toward justice rather than simply keep people alive to continue to live in situations of injustice.

We agree with these principles. Our involvement with numerous conflicts in recent years, however, leads us to conclude that whereas peace cannot exist without justice, it is also true that justice is subverted or negated by the purposes or methods (or both) of many of today's wars. To assume that people who fight always do so for important reasons worthy of our support is simply wrong. In this chapter we describe what we have seen and heard in many societies in conflict that leads us to make this claim.

Before we proceed it is important to make one definitional distinction: The conflict we challenge is violent, destructive conflict. Some people use the word *conflict* to refer to healthy disagreements and struggles. For ease of discourse we use the term to mean negative, unhealthy, usually violent interactions.

This chapter is organized in five parts. We look first at motivations for war and cite examples that question the assumption that root causes of wars are always noble. We also question the depth and breadth of popular support for war as an effective instrument. We then examine a range of characteristics of many recent wars that challenge the use of violence to achieve just outcomes. This is followed by a discussion of who gains and who loses in today's wars and a reflection on why and how wars, even though unpopular and manipulated, continue. We end by discussing why it is important that aid workers understand these issues and carefully and accurately assess the forces at work in the conflict situations in which they provide aid.

Why Wars Are Fought

Wars are fought for good and bad reasons, and most combine a mix of both. Understanding the balance between conflicting motivations—ranging from lofty shared purpose to selfish personal aggrandizement—is critical for aid workers who wish to untangle the ways their aid influences and interacts with conflict.

War as Purposeful

Most people believe "war is hell" and should be avoided—but not at all costs because some goals are worth fighting and dying for. They believe societies should use available diplomatic and political avenues to attain a desired end, but if those avenues fail war as a last resort is an effective instrument through which to achieve ends that cannot be achieved in any other way.

Thus we often speak of the root causes of war. We try to identify what people are really fighting for or fighting about, what makes their sacrifices worthwhile.

Through wars, people have successfully overthrown oppressive regimes, stopped rapacious aggressors, changed land tenure patterns, and achieved greater political and economic justice. Wars of liberation, peasant revolutions, and the Allied Forces' victory over Hitler are examples of wars fought for widely agreed ends.

Another View of War

People also fight, die, and kill—or send others to do so—for purposes that are ignoble and not based on justice. Across the world today many civilians, and many fighters as well, are accusing their leaders of involving them in unjust wars. In Zagreb in 1994 a Croatian woman told us, "We have problems here, of course, but this war is not about these problems. This war is being manipulated by certain people who want power and wealth for themselves. They get rich and the people suffer. These are not admirable 'leaders.' They do not represent the kind of society most of us want to live in."

This theme is repeated in country after country as people explain their wars. The words *manipulation, greed,* and *personal power* arise again and again. In Afghanistan, Somalia, Liberia, Rwanda, Tajikistan, and Bosnia and Herzegovina—to cite only some examples—people describe the processes through which they have been led to fight wars that rather than addressing and solving the problems in their societies have worsened injustice and poverty and deeply undermined the sociopolitical structures. Many wars, today and in the past, are characterized by the absence or erosion of a root cause and hence also of broad popular commitment to that cause or to a clear sense of what can justify an end to the fighting. Wars today are rarely started by poor and marginalized people united in battle as an expression of their deep-seated striving for a just society.

Proximate Causes Are More Important Than Root Causes

We can often gain a better understanding of why people fight wars by looking for proximate rather than root causes. What have we found about the proximate causes of recent wars?

Many post–Cold War conflicts have had their origins in the disruption of power relationships and the resultant political, social, and economic uncertainty that followed the breakup of the Soviet Union and the systems of international and internal control that had existed since the end of World War II. Either because the collapse of the Soviet bloc opened opportunities for new political activities and alignments in countries formerly linked to that bloc or because the contest of U.S.-USSR hegemonies was no longer played out in the arena of other countries, in many areas of the world former, familiar structures of governance collapsed.

In an open field for internal political aspirations, individuals and groups emerged eager to establish new systems and structures. They engaged in a political struggle for leadership—a process encouraged by the disappearance of external control and interest.

Rather than appeal to a constituency by enunciating a set of principles to shape a better future society, however, many of these contenders for power chose to identify with, and appeal for support from, subgroups within the society. They looked into their national histories and selected characteristics that differentiated people from each other. They "reminded" people (sometimes accurately, often with false exaggerations) of historical separations along lines of subgroup identities. In some cases intergroup antagonisms had existed for many years and, with the disappearance of state or other mechanisms for controlling them, were ripe for reexcitement.

Then, importantly, those who sought power in these circumstances convinced people that there was no way to share power with other groups. They propounded a notion of society in which a group either dominates or is dominated. They eschewed as impossible any system of coexistence, cooperation, and power sharing. Often, they intentionally provoked an intergroup crisis or flashpoint to demonstrate that their "dominate or be dominated" philosophy was real. This is how people describe their manipulation into war.

Mixed Motives

Some people cite lofty purposes and root causes as the reasons for every war. "Leaders" always claim a high purpose. Conflicts often embody elements of both principle and self-aggrandizement. Sometimes the initial purposefulness of war changes, and the war itself becomes the reason for future fighting.

An Afghan colleague, reflecting on that country's war, noted that it has had several distinct stages. He viewed the war against the Soviet Union as a jihad (holy war), with a just goal (freedom from an outside invader) unachievable through any other means. When the Soviet forces withdrew, he identified the continued fighting as a "second war" with no purpose except to feed the power hunger of contending leaders and warlords. He felt this second war was "unholy because it is wrong for Muslims to fight Muslims." Things changed again when the newly emergent Taliban militia undertook its ideologically informed campaign to take over and remake the country. This war, although originally driven by purposefulness, deteriorated again into reliance on force to achieve personal power. The conflict has been criticized by many Afghans because it continues to inflict such high costs on civilian populations and has not brought peace. Others have criticized it for establishing a sociopolitical system that denies both equality for women and the personal freedom and human rights of both men and women, enforcing a narrow set of values on the country as a whole through violence and public humiliation. Although the leaders and fighters are religiously and ideologically motivated, support for their definition of justice is widely rejected by the population they seek to rule.

Some wars continue that began under Cold War circumstances. Although the superpower context that prompted those wars has disappeared, a vestige of former ideological positions still characterizes the factions. Continuing tensions in Angola, Guatemala, and El Salvador retain some of the historical purpose that originally motivated them. In each of these cases, however, local analysts report that violent incidents are often perpetrated by groups of bandits who lay claim to familiar ideological positions to "appear" to have a purpose other than their own enrichment. In Nicaragua and Tajikistan, we have been told that members of some of the gangs that operate in the countryside are people who formerly fought against each other. In the postwar period they have joined interests as bandits, thus belying any current pursuit of justice. They continue to fight simply because fighting has become their way of life and livelihood.

Most would agree some wars are motivated by a root cause. The Palestinian-Israeli conflict and the struggles of East Timor–Indonesia, Northern Ireland–England, the Tamils in Sri Lanka, and the Kurds in Turkey and Iraq—to name a few—represent historical contests for political rights and an end to oppressive relationships.

Even in these struggles, however, civilian voices for negotiated compromise are heard. Many on both sides reject the hardened positions of the past and express readiness to agree on territories and political arrangements, land, and power. They say they are ready to leave behind the incessant killing, the cycle of revenge and reprisal, and the repeated displacement of communities as counterproductive to the goal of a just and peaceful world in which they wish to live.

Thus our experiences, combined with what we have heard from many local people in conflict areas in recent years, lead us to conclude that wars are not always or entirely fought to address root causes. Mixed motives and uneven commitments characterize most wars. Often, there is at best a tenuous link between war and justice as its motive.

Other Characteristics of Recent Wars

Other common characteristics among many recent conflicts further challenge the link of warfare to the pursuit of justice.

Civilian-Based Civil War

The majority of today's wars are fought within national boundaries rather than between nations or states. They are fought between groups that have a history of living together and share a language, religion, and culture. They are fought by people who have worked together, been educated together, and sometimes intermarried. People at war today are fighting former friends, neighbors, coworkers, coworshippers, and sometimes even family members.

Civilian-based civil wars are fought in everyday living spaces. The outdoor café, the intervillage bus, the weekend marketplace become

Few would dispute that the struggle in South Africa was driven by a desire for justice for and inclusion of the majority black population. To some people's surprise, as the South Africa Truth Commission held hearings on crimes committed during the apartheid years, it received testimony from black freedom fighters who felt that although their cause was just, their actions in pursuit of justice were "crimes." When they killed children, even in a good cause, they knew their impure means did not fit the pure end they sought. These individuals came forward to confess to the nation and ask for clemency for their actions.

battlegrounds, targeted because they are the places in which civilians live and work. Older people and younger children are absorbed into war both as targets and combatants. In many villages of today's warring societies, young boys carry weapons almost as big as they are.

Today's wars also produce gangs that take advantage of the attendant lawlessness to threaten, rob, rape, and kill common people. Although these gangs may fight for one side, they are rarely fully under the control of the structures of war, so it is difficult to predict when they will follow the orders of the commanders who nominally preside over them. They are organized by and are primarily loyal to the members of their own group and very often operate with impunity and recklessness toward others in their society.

Even conflicts many agree are driven by the pursuit of justice—those in which groups have been denied statehood or civic rights—are increasingly characterized by methods that challenge their linkage to just ends. When freedom fighters blow up the marketplace at which women shop for food; when armies coerce or entice children as young as eight and ten years of age to carry and use powerful weapons; when brutality, torture, and terror (such as beheadings, mutilations, the rape of young children, or the gruesome display of mangled victims) become the methods employed to pursue a just cause, they undermine the justification for that cause.

Perhaps it seems purist to argue that an intrinsic link exists between means and ends, but we are not alone in thinking so. We have heard Tamils and Sinhalese, Irish and English, Palestinians and Israelis, and others locked in combat express horror and disgust at the techniques sometimes used on their behalf. It seems true that the sociopolitical outcomes of wars may reflect both the mixed motives that prompted them to begin and the horrific methods used in their pursuit. If honor and codes of conduct ever made war less brutal and more just, they have been seriously eroded by fighting factions that routinely disregard and disrespect them.

Many of today's wars have erupted quickly. Rather than a last resort after all other avenues for change have been tried, war has been rushed into, often in an effort to preempt power before others seize it. A plethora of portable, easily hidden, and also lethal small arms and "light" weapons supports an easy resort to violence. Many of today's wars are not preceded by failed diplomatic and mediating efforts.

The absorption of civilians and civilian life into warfare as both combatants and primary targets challenges the claim that wars promote justice. The methods employed by many who fight undermine any intrinsic linkage of violent means and good causes. The apparent ease with which people resort to killing for a cause, rather than engaging others in a search for the common good or a mutually acceptable solution, weakens the connection between the use of violence and the achievement of justice.

These common characteristics of many recent and ongoing wars delink them from the pursuit of justice. This is our judgment based on numerous observations. More important, it is also the judgment of many individuals we have met who are themselves engaged in conflict.

Who Gains and Who Loses from Warfare?

The relation of war to the pursuit of justice is further challenged when we examine the gains and losses from warfare. Some people gain from war; however, those gains are narrowly enjoyed, whereas the costs are spread broadly and deeply.

Economic gains are enjoyed by warlords whose personal coffers are enriched by territorial conquest, theft, and taxation. Warriors and gangs of thugs also use the power of their weapons to gain personal wealth. Arms merchants benefit from more, and more prolonged, wars—especially the producers and sellers of small arms and other types of weapons used to terrorize civilians in today's wars. The business and gains of arms production and sales reach into many spheres. Governments of producing countries have supported the marketing efforts of their privately owned arms industries both to avoid sectoral unemployment and to maintain the capacity for arms production in the event they again go to war.

As we discuss more fully in Chapter 4, incomes and profits are also made by people who care for the victims of war. The number of aid agencies and the reliance on those agencies as conduits for the transfer of sometimes massive resources have increased dramatically since

In the postwar period in Colombia and Guatemala, representation in local mediation councils was organized solely through the guerrilla movement and the government. This meant that some indigenous Indian communities that had not been clearly allied with either side (although they had frequently been objects of and sometimes participants in the violence), had no voice in postconflict planning. By some accounts, the decision to include only guerrilla and government representatives weakened the more moderate and conciliatory aspects of local civil society and influenced postwar programming. For example, the exclusion of community people in the planning forum meant programs were designed to reinsert soldiers into society, but no attention was given to how local communities could help them to reintegrate (likely a far more effective strategy for achieving demobilization).

the late 1970s. People in conflict areas who control the resources or have the skills needed by the aid community can benefit from the injection of monies for humanitarian aid prompted by conflict-related crises.

Whereas the wealth to be gained through war is concentrated among a few groups, the losses are widespread and broadly experienced. Destruction of property affects individual families and owners and entire communities and nations. Death, maiming, and loss of health exact both indirect and direct costs. Lost capacity to work and earn has indirect consequences for families and national productivity that last for years. Direct expenses related to recovery and rehabilitation are borne by individuals, families, and communities. Crop losses, destruction of equipment, damaged infrastructure, the abandonment of fields and homes and other places of production, the disruption of production enterprises and processes, the interruption of markets—the list of war-induced economic losses is long.

There are also social and political gains and losses from warfare. In all wars political power becomes identified with military power (at least for a time). The group or individual that prevails militarily also prevails politically and socially. A successful war of liberation may establish inclusive, democratic systems from which everyone can be said to gain, but as discussed earlier, such wars are rare. Groups of fighters often comment on the camaraderie they experience with other members of their forces. Bravery, the importance of sacrifice and risk, and the interdependence that comes from fighting side by side do provide a strong sense of belonging and can be seen as social gains enjoyed by participants in war. When these "gains" define a group that enacts terror on the general population, however, the cost to others is high.

When military preeminence is maintained by individuals or groups that seek their own advantage over the establishment of just and inclusive systems, the political and social gains from war are biased and exclusive. Warlords gain power over land and people, as well as resources. In addition, they may gain international recognition through interviews on the BBC and CNN and invitations to negotiating tables in European capitals. Too often, such recognition more closely reflects the extent of violence these leaders have been able to promote than the legitimacy—or popularity—of their cause. "Politics" can become only a code word for battlefield outcomes.

When no side can achieve a military advantage, wars can be waged for years, deeply fragmenting social systems and causing many to suffer. Lawlessness and thuggery lead to a loss of social cohesion within the broader society.

Even when one side wins a war and thus enjoys some political and social gains, the winners also experience social losses. Many suffer trauma, depression, and dislocation. And as we have seen earlier, when wars have been pursued for questionable motives or through brutal means, their end does not necessarily lead to the establishment of just systems. Legacies of mistrust and intergroup hatred characterize the politics and social systems of many societies that have lived through recent civil wars. The fact that power is determined by weaponry rather than justice, combined with war's legacies of mistrust, fear, hatred, and trauma, challenges any easy assumption that conflict and justice are directly linked.

Why Do Wars Continue?

If all we claim is true, if so many people are uncommitted to the cause of their wars or, if committed, nonetheless eager to find non-war alternatives for pursuing their goals, why do wars continue? Again we report what we have seen and been told in a number of societies in which conflict is active.

Wars Are Self-Perpetuating

Once a war starts, a number of processes make it difficult for it to end. When people have direct and personal experiences of war with their former neighbors, when they or a friend have suffered an atrocity at the

> "People without arms, without any real power outside of their personal authority had to move to the sidelines.... They kept quiet because the 'irreconcilables' will do anything. The 'irreconcilables' know that if the federal authorities succeed in establishing control, they will be called to account. So there's nothing left for them to do but fight."
>
> "I think that if the militants don't leave those villages, [another] ... one [will] ... be destroyed.... And the 'irreconcilables' will probably be able to provoke a bombing or artillery attack very easily."
>
> —Interviews with Chechens by Joan Beecher, reporter for Voice of America, filed in a report from Chechnya on February 26, 1996

hands of people with whom they once lived and interacted, they begin to subscribe to the exclusionary philosophy expounded by their "leaders." They wonder how they could have trusted "those people" and conclude that they can never trust them again.

Equally important in perpetuating a civil war is the too-common experience of having committed an atrocity against a former friend, neighbor, or colleague. Sometimes the atrocity was as simple as having done nothing to help when someone was threatened or attacked; sometimes it involved face-to-face violence. In either case, guilt is strong. When good people commit acts they cannot believe they would have committed against someone they have known, they often feel compelled to justify the action. If "they" are doing horrible things to us and we can no longer trust "them," then an act against "them" can be interpreted as necessary.

Warfare itself, especially when civilians are targeted, produces a cycle of actions that perpetuate themselves. Action, reaction, violation, and retribution feed a cycle that becomes more and more difficult to break. The experience of war increasingly becomes a root cause that leads to future wars.

Warfare that continues over a number of years can leave a generation of young people who know no other vocation and have no civilian skills. They can find no other employment and thus have an interest in continued fighting. It is difficult for society to reintegrate them, and their lawlessness and banditry perpetuate a general mistrust and suspicion that can create broader tensions.

In addition, some individuals and groups, although they enjoy no direct economic, political, or social gains, nonetheless perpetuate wars. Some people become so strongly identified with a cause and make such sacrifices for that cause that its ending represents a threat to their identity. Motivated originally by the nobility of the cause, such people may

A formerly rejectionist group finally agreed to engage directly in peace talks with a long-fought enemy. A bomb shattered a market just hours before the critical first talks were to open. Neither side accused the other; both met at the appointed hour.

A close analyst of the situation was interviewed on international radio later in the day. He cited the significance of this forward motion, commenting on the importance of maintaining the momentum toward peace in the face of the bombing.

But the reporter later asked, "What, if anything, might undo this effort toward peace?" The expert responded, "Another bombing will surely undo it." He thus signaled that two bombings would be successful even though one had failed to disrupt the peace process.

become rejectionists. They often commit actions their constituencies abhor but that feed the momentum for reprisal rather than for the achievement of a just peace.

Warfare also engenders irreconcilables. Sometimes people who suffer want only to inflict pain on others in return for pain they have experienced. Sometimes people have committed such crimes during war that if peace were to come they would be tried for their actions. For these people an end to war represents their undoing; a continuation of war is the only means by which they can survive.

Although they may represent a small group numerically, the rejectionists and the irreconcilables are important impediments to peace. Experience shows that as progress is made toward negotiation, these groups often feel sufficiently threatened to take direct action to unravel its achievement. In most societies moving from warfare to cease-fire to peace, at least one and sometimes repeated attempts occur to undo the peace. Assassinations of leaders engaged in negotiation or a violent act that rekindles intergroup mistrust can rally public opinion and fear and cause peace talks to be cancelled and hostilities resumed.

These actions are predictable and thus should be ineffective. Too often, however, peacemakers appear surprised by rejectionist-irreconcilable violence and allow it to interrupt steps that have been carefully constructed to bring the majority to agreement. When they do so, the actions succeed. When peacemakers signal rejectionists that their disruptions will undermine momentum toward peace, they reinforce rejectionists' resolve to carry out such acts. Every time a rejectionist act of violence succeeds in ending a peace process, other rejectionists are encouraged to commit their own acts of terrorism. The cycle is self-reinforcing.

Diaspora

Another group that sometimes perpetuates war and makes peace more difficult includes people who are related to the area in which a conflict is under way but who live in another location, the diaspora communities. Sometimes these people fled when war erupted and established themselves as an exiled group (e.g., the Tuaregs in Norway, the Tamils in Europe). In other cases they were born outside the conflict area (e.g., Irish born in the United States, Jews living outside of Israel) but have been raised with a strong identity for the cause represented in a regional struggle.

> Two Jewish women were interviewed by a U.S. reporter as the Palestinian Authority's administration in the Gaza Strip began under the terms of the Oslo peace accords. One lived in New York City, the other in a settlement in the northern Gaza Strip. The first was incensed: "Jews living in Gaza must stay. They must insist that Israel provide troops to defend them. They must hold true to the dream. We conquered that land; we must keep it!"
>
> The second woman laughed: "Why should we continue to live on a piece of land here in Gaza that has been negotiated to belong to the Palestinians just because someone in New York thinks we should? It is easy for her to insist that we hang on. I am ready to move back into Israel and raise my children. If we're ever going to live in peace, we have to make some compromises. Of course I loved my home in Gaza. I am sorry that I am one of the people who has to move. But if this is the way to peace, then let's get on with it."

Such groups may use their positions to raise money to support warfare. They may enlist public opinion and international political action on behalf of the cause. And sometimes they become even more rigid in their demands for the conditions for peace than their fellow countrypeople who live in the war setting. Even when local groups may be ready to negotiate, those outside the daily threat of war assume purist positions, insisting on a peace they imagine to be best.

Habits of War: The Mind-Set of War

Habits and mind-sets alone cannot make war continue, but they often cause people to miss opportunities to move away from war and toward

> In Lebanon as the first months of the cease-fire held and people began to believe in the peace, the staff of a local NGO and an outside consultant considered how to reshape the NGO's program to make the transition from relief to development. A general malaise affected the group, which found little inspiration in its new work and did not respond to the consultant's proddings. Finally, the staff director said: "I know what's wrong. I know why we are having trouble getting into this discussion: Every day for the past fifteen years we have gotten up and gone to work not knowing whether today would be our last. Many of our friends and colleagues have been killed. We knew we could be caught in cross fire at any moment. We taught ourselves to live in the moment and never to consider even the next hour, much less the next week or year! Now in the peace we have to plan ahead. We have to think in entirely different ways. We have to take small steps to build, over a long time, to a future development. We don't know how to plan and work for peace!"

peace. Some people in warring societies reflect on the way violence permeates social relationships. They note that in a context where random or willful violence is common life becomes less valued, and people quickly resort to arms rather than discussion or negotiation to "settle" disputes. In particular, we frequently hear a concern about the values children learn when they are raised in a context of conflict. In Afghanistan, for example, parents and local aid workers frequently comment on the pervasiveness of the "culture of violence" that shapes expectations regarding interpersonal interactions. Some local NGOs are introducing programs that directly challenge this culture and attempt to reteach both the values and processes of peaceful social interaction.

In addition, in many conflict settings aid workers have reflected on the processes by which they, too, are swept up in the acceptance of warfare. With admirable introspection and honesty, some have described the excitement of working for a good cause under fire. They talk of the spirit engendered by danger and how people care for and relate to each other in deeply meaningful ways. The mind-set of war can blind aid workers to important opportunities to support local people's disengagement from conflict.

Aid workers—and aid agencies—sometimes place higher value on work done in war than on work in nonwar societies. Prestige, the power to sway agency opinion, and even staff promotions are sometimes linked to war work rather than to peacetime or postconflict work.

> In Sarajevo as the IFOR troops (peace implementation forces) moved into positions across Bosnia and Herzegovina, a visitor interviewed an aid worker who had been in the city for over two years and had seen the worst of the siege. The interviewer asked, "How do you feel now that the fighting has ended?"
>
> The aid worker answered: "To tell you the truth, we don't know what to do with ourselves. When new aid people arrive, we feel superior to them. We lived through it. They cannot understand. We tell stories of the war as if it represented reality and as if peace is unreal and less important. We tell our 'war stories' of time in the bomb shelters, and we almost forget how frightened we were. We can't find any excitement in this work. It's very strange to realize this."

Why It Is Important for Aid Workers to Understand War

Because aid becomes a part of the context and hence of the wars in which it is given, aid workers need to understand the motivations and purposes of the conflicts where they work. They need to hear the varied voices of people in warring societies and to assess the breadth (or lack thereof) of commitment to a cause and the validity and historical genuineness (or lack thereof) of cited purposes.

How do people in the conflict society feel about the conflict? Are they committed to a cause of justice, or do they feel manipulated by leaders seeking power? Which people express which attitudes? Who gains and who loses in the context of this conflict? Is everyone embroiled in the war, or do parts of the country live in relative peace?

These are some of the questions aid workers should consider based on what we have found and heard in conflict areas during recent years. To enter a conflict with assumptions based on an ideal of justice is to risk making program mistakes. Knowledge of the common characteristics and important differences discussed earlier provides a starting point for listening to local opinions and identifying opportunities for reinforcing connections rather than divisions among people.

The opportunities for aid to reinforce war or nonwar vary over time. A number of civilian-based civil wars, however, seem to have three stages. These stages are not fixed or even necessarily sequential. That is, the course of warfare can sometimes cause a surprising shift in attitudes, and we also find that some people in a war zone may be in what we think of as phase 1 while others may be in phase 2 or 3. We report the three stages observed in some wars, however, because thinking about them can alert aid workers to the different opportunities that occur over time so that aid can have optimal impact.

A group of aid workers in southern Sudan was analyzing the war there. They concluded, "There are really three wars here. The 'real' war is the war between the north and south. This war matters because it deals with the freedom of two different groups to live within the same political structures. It requires a political solution, and we have little power to affect this except as we pressure our agencies to take on advocacy roles.

"But there is also the south-south war between factions that split. This has much more to do with competition between different leaders who want to be in power than it does with the issues that underlie the north-south war. Furthermore, there are the inter-village 'cattle raids' or, really, thugisms.

"It is easy for people to think all of the fighting is directly linked to the north-south conflict and that nothing can be done about any of it until that war is ended. Many people believe both the south-south battles and even the raids are part of the same war. But if we see that there are really three wars, we can also see how our aid reinforces and feeds them. The south-south conflict and the cattle raids occur in our space—the places where we are giving aid—and they often have to do with the resources we are providing. We can change this. We can figure out new ways to give aid so we don't reinforce these two wars."

The group's separation of a conflict into its different parts helped its members to see immediate ways they could change their programs to be more effective. Later in other sessions, aid staff who work in Sudan identified programmatic approaches to address the issues of the north-south war as well. For example, there are north-south linkages in regular systems of cattle trading. Also, shifts in alliances mean people on both sides share tribal affiliations and religions. For example, there are large numbers of Dinka people on both sides. Aid programs could be designed to reinforce those connections in ways that encourage a move toward, and the stability of, a future political settlement.

When the first violence is occurring many people say, "What are we doing to ourselves? We've lived together for years. This is insane. Surely this must stop." But after some months of warfare, personal experiences of horror and suffering grow. At this second stage many people become convinced that they cannot trust the other side and that they must win the war. In many conflicts, even in this stage when people are committed to winning, some will openly acknowledge that the war is driven by political leaders seeking personal gain. They are committed to victory even though they recognize that victory and justice are not equivalent.

Finally, in a third stage many people can be heard to say, "This is absurd. What are we doing to ourselves? We lived together before; we can live together again. Anything is better than this." People are exhausted from the war and recognize that it has lost meaning in any ideological sense. The pursuit of war ceases to be worth the sacrifice.

We have found no pattern and thus no way to predict why some civil wars continue for many years and other societies achieve a readiness for peace in a shorter period of time. As noted earlier, some parts of a country or some people in a country may be in one of the three stages while other parts or people are in another stage. The ways aid workers can link with people who are ready to disengage from conflict and help them to find ways to do so are different and perhaps more obvious in the first and third stages than in the second stage. (At all stages, aid workers should be alert to ways aid might be reinforcing tensions or divisions among groups and thus feeding into conflict.) Listening to local people's attitudes toward the fighting is important as aid workers identify opportunities to support disengagement.

3

Characteristics of Conflict Areas

Conflict situations are characterized by intergroup tensions and divisions. Everyone knows this, expects it, and focuses on it.

More interesting is the fact that conflict situations are also characterized by local capacities for peace and by connectors that interlink the people who fight. This surprises many people—indeed, it surprised us as we became familiar with numerous conflict situations.

When international aid workers enter conflict zones, they tend naturally to focus on the conflict. They have been cautioned by family and friends and been instructed to guard their own safety. When well prepared they have been counseled on how to handle personal stress and trauma. When they arrive on-site they see the violence because its manifestations are immediate and powerful.

Local people in conflict settings also tend to focus on divisions and tensions. The newness of the violence and the constant danger it poses overwhelm them. Even though they may maintain "normal" actions (which often represent connectors, as we discuss later), they see everything as "abnormal" because of the conflict. They often fail to recognize the many ways they continue to act and think in nonwar ways.

The most important lesson learned through the Local Capacities for Peace Project (LCPP) is that of the existence and strength of peace capacities and connectors. In all civil war situations some things connect the people who fight. In all societies there are capacities for peace.

Too often, when international assistance providers arrive in a conflict area, they are so overwhelmed by the violence that they fail to see or recognize the capacities for peace. The loud and compelling terms of war—violence, danger, and expressions of hatred—are accepted as the only reality. As a result, aid is often provided in relation to the divisions in the society rather than in relation to and support of the connectors. Aid can thus inadvertently reinforce conflict and miss remarkable opportunities for helping people to rediscover and strengthen the aspects of their lives that connect them to each other.

In this chapter we examine both the local capacities for peace and the divisions that exist in societies in conflict. To counter a prevalent bias toward concentrating on the causes and manifestations of war (early warning systems, needs assessments), we first discuss local capacities for peace.

Capacities for Peace and Connectors

Even in virulent warfare, more people do not fight than do so. More individuals do not kill their neighbors than do so. More societies avoid warfare than engage in it. More would-be leaders fail to arouse people to violence than succeed in doing so. More people strive to correct their societies' systems of marginalization and injustice through nonwar means than through warfare.

People generally tend at least as much to avoid and avert violence as they do to seek and pursue it. Even in today's troubled world, peace is more widespread than war.

The Local Capacities for Peace Project found that even in societies where civilian-based civil war rips daily patterns apart, many aspects of life continue to connect people rather than divide them. Common history, culture, language, and experience; shared institutions and values; economic and political interdependence; and habits of thinking and acting exist in all societies, including those embroiled in civil war.

In addition, all societies have systems for handling disagreements and tensions without violence. Often they designate specific categories of people, such as elders or women, as negotiators or reconcilers. All have systems for limiting and ending violence if it erupts, and all have individuals who assert the values of peace even when prevalent warfare makes such positions unpopular and dangerous.

All of these elements constitute local capacities for peace. They exist prior to war and often avert open violence. Obviously, they are not always sufficient to prevent war. But even when war erupts, local capacities for peace exist; in fact, some are aroused by the experience of war. Peace capacities are important because they provide the base on which future peace can and must be built. They are the existing—and potential—building blocks of systems of political and economic interaction that can ensure stable, peaceful, and just futures for societies once in conflict.

We have identified five categories of peace capacities and the connectors (later we discuss these categories as they relate to war capacities and the dividers): systems and institutions, attitudes and actions, shared values and interests, common experiences, and symbols and occasions. These are not airtight, mutually exclusive categories; rather, they often overlap or run into each other. We include all five categories to illustrate the range of connectors found to exist. We hope to raise awareness among aid workers of where to look for peace capacities and how to recognize opportunities to support them.

Systems and Institutions

In all societies in which civil war breaks out, markets continue to connect people across the lines of the fighting. Sometimes a system of interenemy trade is formalized involving contracts and third-country bank accounts. Sometimes trade occurs at the traditional Saturday morning market where women gather with their homegrown wares. Markets can represent places where people who are divided by war meet and interact, maintaining relationships they value. Or they may represent only an organized method of distributing needed goods and, for some, of making profits. In any case, they always exist.

> The man who ran a tea shop in the market on the outskirts of Sarajevo was interviewed. "This market continued throughout the war," he said. "Oh yes, I'll sit and sip tea with 'them' in the daytime and take their money, but I may go out tonight to shoot them."

Infrastructure also continues to connect people in civil war societies. Electrical, water, and communications systems and roads can connect warring people who jointly depend on them and thus let them remain even in the midst of war.

Some institutions continue to have importance for all sides even though they are fighting. Communications systems, for example, can provide linkages among people at war. In many war zones we have been told that for those on all sides the BBC represents a source of the truth about what is happening. People appreciate knowing that they and those on the "other side" are hearing the same news. In Tusla a group set up a room filled with computers so they could maintain E-mail contact with colleagues and friends on the Serb side when fighting had separated them.

Systems and institutions may bring people into direct contact (as in markets and personal communication systems), or they may connect people without any direct, face-to-face interaction (such as the BBC and the electrical grids). In either event they provide connection and continuity even when people are divided in conflict.

I stood on the border of southern Tajikistan and Afghanistan and saw overhead an enormous and complex grid of electrical wires. All around me were large craters in the ground, created when shells fell during the recent fighting. I asked how they had rebuilt the electricity so quickly.

"The electricity was never destroyed," they responded.

I laughed. "So the aim was not so good," I joked, thinking the shells had simply failed to reach their true target.

"Oh no," they said, "we never intended to destroy the electricity. We agreed that we all needed it."

Later, when I drove from Split along the road to Sarajevo, I also saw a destroyed village—completely burned out—and overhead the wires for electricity. Not mentioning my Tajikistan experience, I asked the same question about how they had rebuilt it so soon. I got the same answer: "No, we never destroyed it; we agreed that we all needed the electricity."

"When I heard the report on the BBC about what my government had done to the Tamils, I lost my stomach for war. I began to look for other ways this awful problem can be resolved."

—Sinhalese woman in private interview

Attitudes and Actions

A second category of connectors is found in people's nonwar attitudes and actions. In the midst of war, some individuals and groups continue to express tolerance, acceptance, and even love or appreciation for people on the other side. They refuse to demonize or stereotype the "others," and they recognize the failures and wrongdoing of their own side.

In Bosnia a few men sat together in the early days of the war. The conversation turned to the war, and they agreed that they could not support the ethnic division their leaders preached. They started a citizens' forum in one of their homes and called a public meeting to see if anyone else felt as they did. Over 2,000 people came to the first meeting. In just over a year the membership grew to over 15,000 people.

In Somalia a young man tells of a time when two clans began to fight. He and his friends, who did not want to take part in the battle because they saw it as meaningless, simply "walked"—that is, they announced their "membership" in a third clan that was not at war with either of the others. They were able to make this shift because over the years there had been so many intermarriages that people actually "belonged" to a number of different clans. They could thus change clans to avoid a foolish fight.

In every conflict area some individuals and groups continue to act in nonwar ways, doing things the war would dictate are wrong. They join people from the other side in associations. In some places professors have set themselves apart from intergroup fighting and continued to publish an academic journal or to hold yearly meetings in their academic discipline. Sometimes people form new associations or institutions to provide a connection when conflict has caused divisions. In Ethiopia, Somalia, Israel, Palestine, and many other places, women have formed associations that involve all sides of a conflict in joint actions for community welfare. Sometimes these groups are focused ex-

In Afghanistan a young man on a bicycle hit a child. The young man was from one clan, the child from another. In the mood of antagonism and reprisal that permeated the countryside, fighters from the two sides gathered on rooftops, armed and ready to fight. People on the streets and in the market below quietly moved into the space between the two assembling groups. They stood and waited. The fighters did not want to kill their neighbors. The standoff allowed enough time to get the clan leaders together; they found another way to settle the dispute over the injured child.

In Tajikistan a Kulyabi woman welcomed her returning Garmi neighbors who had fled when their side lost the war in Khatlon Province. She gave them salt and bread, a traditional symbol of hospitality, and invited them to her home for dinner. She cooked for three days and sat her returning neighbors and her Kulyabi neighbors across the table from each other. They ate together in what she hoped was a spirit of reconciliation.

> In Afghanistan two factions were gathering in a village face-off. The mullah took out his bullhorn and ran into the street. He shouted that no one would come to the funerals of those who died in this battle and that they would not die as martyrs. Everyone knew what his admonition meant—namely, that those who died in this battle would not go to paradise. The battle did not occur.

> In Somalia during the height of the war, a number of villages unilaterally decided they did not want to participate. It was not their battle. They defined their boundaries as an area without war, a "pocket of peace." If people came into these areas to recruit young men to fight, the community would expel them. In one case the community arrested the war recruiters, tried them, and executed them for violating the local laws.

plicitly on peacemaking; sometimes they bring people together for activities not directly related to the conflict.

People rescue children of the other side when they find them in danger, sometimes adopting them for the duration of the war. They step in to save people from the other side who are threatened by their side. Many stories of such heroism are heard in Rwanda, Bosnia and Herzegovina, India and Pakistan, and all war areas. In the midst of terrible conflict people (sometimes many people) quietly refuse to participate; they may take direct action against the violence and—as is seen in every civil war—perform heroic personal acts to save people from the other side from injury and death, often eliciting their own injury and death by doing so.

These nonwar attitudes and actions may be taken consciously by an individual or a group in protest against the conflict. Or they may simply be expressed in the course of daily living because in the immediate sense they seem "normal" or "right."

Shared Values and Interests

When people have an interest in continuing a system (even when it is also used by the enemy), as in the examples of electric and health services cited earlier, or when they share a common value, such as a love for children, these commonalities can represent connectors in conflict

In Sarajevo a Muslim woman told the interviewers: "When the shelling started, my Serb neighbor and I would check on each other's children. If she was away I would take her child to the shelter with me. When I was gone I knew she would take my son and daughter with her. We had been friends before. We couldn't let the fighting end it."

societies. The United Nations Children's Fund (UNICEF) has successfully negotiated "days of tranquillity" and "corridors of peace" in which all sides in warring areas agree to facilitate inoculations of children. Neither side wants its children to die of preventable diseases, and thus each is often willing to let children from the other side also receive care. In southern Sudan, aid agency staff report that for some time health workers were allowed to cross lines when food providers were not because people accepted everyone's right to receive health services.

Common Experiences

A shared experience—even the experience of war—can provide a basis for linkage and connection among people on differing sides of a conflict. Women often empathize with women on the other side, citing the commonalities of their and their families' suffering. In Central America one NGO started a postwar production plant in which workers were recruited from among the wounded fighters in the recently ended war. One employee commented, "Once you've lost a leg, you're all alike. It doesn't matter anymore what side you fought on."

In Bosnia and Herzegovina convoy drivers who delivered goods under dangerous circumstances report that they often kept in touch with drivers on the other side. They were able to talk through their radio systems, and they developed a kind of brotherhood in which they shared information about road conditions, impending danger, and other factors.

When the war ended, some of these drivers sought out their counterparts from the other side. They wanted to meet these individuals who had become colleagues through the worst period of the war. Although their ethnicity might have made them enemies, their common experience—and the help they gave to each other—overcame divisions and created new connections.

In Beirut during the heaviest fighting, all schools were closed, and children spent hours in bomb shelters with their families. UNICEF was concerned about the loss of schooling over many months and also about the psychological stress these children were experiencing. One staff person started a children's educational magazine named *SAWA*, which in Arabic means "together." She and her colleagues began to print and distribute a booklet of stories, math problems, geography, and history to children across Lebanon. They left the two center pages of the magazine blank and invited children to use them to draw a picture or write a story or poem to share with other children. They were soon inundated with contributions, which they printed in subsequent editions. Through this publication, which reached all children, UNICEF built on the common experience of all Lebanese families and provided a new connection among them.

In Bosnia and Herzegovina one of the earliest effective ways aid agencies supported reconnections among people of different ethnicities within towns and cities was through small orchestras, choirs, academic journals, and youth clubs. Musicians, academics, and young people were eager to resume normal activities and to reengage in areas in which they had special interests and talents. They were ready to reform associations of these common efforts with people who had only recently been "the enemy."

In Burundi, rather than import the words of the already formulated International Humanitarian Principles to which it is committed, the International Committee of the Red Cross brought together a group of Burundians, representing different groups and strata of society, to consider where in their own culture they could identify the aphorisms and cultural values that conveyed humanitarian principles. Over some months the group collected and organized sayings and myths shared across Burundi society and took them "on the road" in plays and performances.

Symbols and Occasions

National art, music, and literature and historic anniversaries, monuments, and ceremonies all provide connections in societies torn apart by civil war. For example, the UNICEF magazine *SAWA* always included an entry on "our national heritage" in which a national monument, historical event, or other aspect of prewar national culture was featured. The intent was to reaffirm the nation of Lebanon in which all people shared a history.

Capacities for War, Sources of Tension, and Dividers

Experience shows that societies at war also have capacities for war and for things that divide people. Although it seems odd to use the word *capacities* when speaking of war, we do so because experience shows that in an attempt to enhance or build on local capacities in conflict settings, aid can inadvertently support those that in a given instance are actively involved in and pursuing warfare. It becomes important to realize that not all capacities in a recipient society are ones we really mean to strengthen.

Capacities for war and dividers are not simply the mirror images of capacities for peace and connectors. Although it is useful to think about the dividers in the same five categories we used to describe the connectors, many of the elements included in each category are fundamentally distinct from those listed previously. It is important to be aware of this difference to stay alert to the reality of any given situation. It is easy to believe, for example, that women's groups are capacities for peace. We have found that in some situations, however, women's groups are active supporters of war; they teach their children to be suspicious of other groups and support their husbands as warriors. In some instances they even take up arms themselves. Similarly, in some situations religion may link people who fight on opposing sides; in other situations religion represents the division around which fighting occurs. Those elements that fall under the headings of capacities for peace should be strikingly different from those identified in a parallel circumstance as capacities for war.

Systems and Institutions

The systems and institutions of violent conflict include armies and gangs, the production and distribution of weapons, and the apparatus of war propaganda. These systems come into existence and develop strength as conflict unfolds.

In addition, societies have systems and institutions that historically or traditionally separate people and thus can cause tension between them. These include systems of discrimination, exclusion, and dominance—often manifested in unequal access to education, health, justice, jobs, or other of society's goods. These systems can include separate religious institutions. They might involve spatial separation, as when different groups occupy different areas of a country (or even a city) or when tensions exist between rural and urban people or groups that earn their livelihood from different sources (e.g., pastoralists and agriculturalists). Such systems and institutions may promote or reflect long-standing tensions between groups and can cause—or be manipulated to cause—conflict.

Attitudes and Actions

Violence, threats, torture, brutality, lawlessness, displacement, and expulsions are war actions that divide people. Once unleashed, they create divisive tensions between groups. Attitudes of mistrust, suspicion, fear, and hatred accompany and are reinforced by such actions. These attitudes and actions are promoted by some of the tools of war, such as war propaganda and the demonization and hence dehumanization of the "other."

Some war attitudes and actions precede open conflict. Prejudice, competition for resources, incidents of hostility, and threats exist in all societies. They may result from systems of discrimination and exclusion or dominance and can be manipulated to promote violence.

Different Values and Interests

Although many values and interests are shared across societies, some also differentiate groups from each other. Interest groups—defined by location, occupation, or other identity—vie for power and resources. Values that represent subcultures and different religious affiliations exist virtually everywhere. Only the most homogeneous societies (of which very few exist) do not experience ongoing tension between subgroups' desire for a distinct identity and their urge for sameness or for achieving equality with all other groups in resources and power.

Another set of conflicting interests that affects, if not underlies, many recent wars involves outside powers who promote or support conflicts in other societies. In some cases outsiders have an interest in who holds power in another country; in others, they are interested only in the continuing instability of the country at war (which for some reason serves the outsider's domestic or security interests).

Different Experiences

Whereas common experiences link people, different experiences can divide them. Perceptions of the world, and of right and wrong, of justice and injustice often reflect direct and immediate experience. When a country's law enforcement system treats different groups differently, for example, one group may see that system as providing safety whereas another group experiences it as threatening. Such differences can create tensions that divide people.

Symbols and Occasions

Finally, whereas national symbols and occasions link people, distinct subgroup symbols and occasions can accentuate differences and excite unease, suspicion, and fear between groups. And they can easily be manipulated to emphasize or create divisions.

Understanding Peace and War
Capacities Is Important

As noted at the beginning of this chapter, if aid providers are aware only of the factors that divide communities and do not recognize and relate to those that link them, their aid can reinforce the former and undermine the latter. Thus it is critical for aid workers to assess what actually links or divides people in the area in which they work. In every society—those at war and those not at war—both connectors and dividers exist. To the extent that they depend on some public support for the pursuit of their cause, "successful" warlords focus attention on dividers and sources of tension as if no connectors exist. Recognition and reemphasis of commonalities and shared values, experiences, and systems can reinforce people's commitment to nonwar problem solving.

It is important not to be romantic about peace capacities and connectors. Whereas in some places women reach across factional lines to reassert the commonality of their families' suffering, in other places women carry the flag for continued conflict, insisting on revenge for the suffering of their loved ones. That is, what may be a capacity for peace in one area may reinforce intergroup divisions in another.

Experience shows that most people embody both capacities for peace and capacities for war. Some warriors are fully committed to con-

In southern Sudan, as a European aid agency was about to launch a new program in health training, the southern movement split into two factions. The aid agency immediately assumed that to be effective it should redesign its program to include two health training centers, one in each faction's region.

Reflecting on this decision later, one agency staff member noted, "We rewarded the split! They got twice as many resources. And because we know that health is the one sector in which at that time international agencies were allowed to operate across lines, I believe we did not have to do this. I wonder what would have happened if we had continued with our original plan of one center. I suspect we would have recruited from both sides and that this center could have represented one place in the society where they could have legitimately met and worked together."

He then thought about how to alter the impact of his agency's aid. He began to develop plans to redesign each of the two training centers. One, he thought, should focus on training public health nurses and the other on training rural paramedics. By offering two distinct training programs, one in each location, he hoped to use his agency's aid to help bring people from both sides together as trainees.

flict, and some peacemakers are wholly committed to peace. Most people, however, sometimes support warfare and sometimes act in nonwar ways; they express both war-reinforcing attitudes and nonwar attitudes. Especially in civil wars, individuals often seem to vacillate between the two.

This suggests that aid interventions have an opportunity to influence the relative prominence of peace or war capacities. If aid supports the systems and institutions of war, those capacities are strengthened. If aid supports the systems and institutions and the attitudes and actions of peace, those capacities can be reinforced. Aid can support either capacity. In subsequent chapters we report in greater detail numerous examples of aid's interaction with both conflict and peace capacities.

One additional point should be considered here. A participant in one LCPP workshop noted, "People who make war are much better at recognizing capacities for peace than we—the aid community—are!" Because they connect people, capacities for peace are often explicitly targeted by warriors. The electrical systems, irrigation networks, and marketplaces that link people become targets for terrorism and destruction. The individual or group who engages in concerted peace actions may be threatened or killed. Shared history, values, and culture

Prior to the war, local nongovernmental organizations were operating in Sarajevo, including Serb, Muslim, Catholic, and Jewish agencies. Although the NGOs had been started by specific groups and served members of their own communities, they also offered services to people of other communities who lived in the part of the city where they operated or had needs they could help meet.

When the war erupted these agencies provided critical emergency aid to war victims. International NGOs, which wanted to remain nonpartisan in relation to the conflict, quickly identified these NGOs as partners and as recipients of their funds. To demonstrate their evenhandedness, however, some external NGOs designated the funds they channeled through each local agency as targeted specifically for the ethnicity identified with that agency—that is, they gave to the Serb NGO for Serbs, to the Muslim NGO for Bosnians, and to the Catholic NGO for Croatians.

Some local NGO leaders later commented that although the external agencies did not create the divisions of the war, their way of targeting aid did reinforce divisions. They wondered aloud whether if the external NGOs had given funds to the group of agencies and had them decide together how to allocate those funds, it might have reinforced and strengthened joint decisionmaking and a common concern for suffering.

are challenged and reinterpreted by war propaganda. For aid providers the challenge is both to recognize capacities for peace and to find appropriate ways to reinforce and support them without simultaneously increasing the probability that they will be targeted and destroyed by those who pursue war.

4

Aid's Impact on Conflict Through Resource Transfers

When international assistance is given in the context of conflict, it both affects and is affected by that conflict. In this chapter and the two that follow, we examine a number of ways in which aid and conflict interact and show how the choices made in aid programming can affect whether the impacts of aid on conflict are negative or positive.

Experience shows that even when it is effective in doing what it is intended to do to save lives or promote development, aid too often also feeds into, reinforces, and prolongs conflicts. Again and again aid workers tell how their aid is distorted by local politics and is misappropriated by warriors to support the war. Again and again war victims report that aid is enriching warlords or strengthening the "enemy." Again and again the systems of aid and the manner in which aid workers interact with conflict reinforce the modes and moods of those at war, undermining and weakening the nonwar aspects of the society.

Why does aid, which is intended to do good, end up doing harm? Is it inevitable that it do so? The answers to these questions can be found in past aid experience. From the examples of aid's negative impacts gathered in many conflict zones around the world, clear and consistent patterns emerge. Although at first each example appears particular and unique—caused and shaped by special, local circumstances—a look at all of the experiences together reveals important similarities.

We are heartened rather than discouraged by the repetitiveness of the negative lessons because where patterns exist it becomes possible to predict how things can go wrong. And if we have enough information and understanding to predict negative patterns, it is also possible to find programming options—other ways of working—that avoid them. From the lessons learned from past aid experience, we are convinced that it is not inevitable that aid exacerbate war. Furthermore, as our discussion in Chapter 3 suggests, a better understanding of the patterns in

> An aid worker said: "We are doing an effective job here. We can document how many lives we are saving with the food and medicines we're bringing in. There is a problem, however. Because we have to cross the border controlled by one faction to reach one of the groups we serve, some of our aid supplies are routinely taken by the soldiers at the crossing. This distresses us because we know these things are being sold to buy weapons or to feed soldiers. But when we think of the people who depend on us to survive, we believe the good we are doing outweighs the harm. It is ironic that we help save lives that are at risk because of the war and, as we do so, our aid also feeds the war that makes people need aid. It just goes around and around."
>
> —Heard with slight variations in many conflict areas, including Liberia, Tajikistan, Bosnia and Herzegovina, Somalia, Sudan, Rwanda, Angola, and others

which aid and conflict interact makes it possible to design aid programs that relate to and support local capacities for peace.

In the discussion that follows, we give examples and identify the patterns by which aid inadvertently reinforces conflict, and we discuss what has been learned about how to avoid this problem. We also look at how aid can be designed to build on and support local capacities for peace.

Our point is not to condemn aid providers for past mistakes or to insist that humanitarian and development assistance agencies take on an additional peacemaking mandate. Rather, our purpose is to enable conscientious aid workers to use what has been learned in the past so they can work more effectively in future complex situations. The mandates of humanitarian and development aid should not change. But given what has been learned, it is not necessary or justified to act as if aid has no responsibility for its negative—or positive—side effects on conflicts. While pursuing humanitarian and developmental imperatives, aid workers should also know and do more to ensure that their aid does no harm. Aid reinforces conflict or strengthens local capacities for peace through the direct and indirect impacts of its resource transfers and through its implicit ethical messages.

•   •   •

Because aid resources represent economic wealth and political power, people engaged in war will always want to control them. It would be odd—even subversive to their cause—if they did not do so. Thus it can be unproductive and naive for aid providers to expect warlords to accept fully the humanitarian principle that victims on all sides of a conflict have equal rights to aid. When the "enemy" receives any support, including humanitarian aid, it is viewed as counter to the sought-after victory. For example, during the Vietnam War the United States restricted all aid shipments to North Vietnam, thereby forcing U.S. NGOs that wanted to work on both sides of the conflict to purchase aid items and ship them through Canada to avoid prosecution under a U.S. Treasury law that prohibited trading with the enemy.

Experience shows that aid's economic and political resources affect conflict in five predictable ways.

1. Aid resources are often stolen by warriors and used to support armies and buy weapons.
2. Aid affects markets by reinforcing either the war economy or the peace economy.
3. The distributional impacts of aid affect intergroup relationships, either feeding tensions or reinforcing connections.
4. Aid substitutes for local resources required to meet civilian needs, freeing them to support conflict.
5. Aid legitimizes people and their actions or agendas, supporting the pursuit of either war or peace.

Theft

Warriors often steal aid goods and use them to finance their war efforts. Stolen food, blankets, vehicles, and communications systems can be used by armies directly or be sold to buy needed supplies. Theft is the most widely recognized process by which aid feeds into conflict (although as the discussion of other processes in the remainder of this chapter will show, it is not necessarily the most important in terms of impact).

To steal, thieves need information about what, where, and when goods are or will be available. They need a location at which they can gain control of the goods (a checkpoint, a narrow road, a warehouse). They need to know enough goods of sufficient value will be available to make the theft worthwhile. They need to be able to "get away with it"— not to be caught or, if caught, not to be held accountable for their actions. Thieves need knowledge, opportunity, incentive, and impunity.

What to Do: Programming Options

Aid workers have been extremely inventive in developing strategies to deter theft. Some aid agencies deliver goods unannounced, episodically, according to no fixed schedule, and never to the same location twice so that thieves lack sufficient knowledge to allow them to steal. Some agencies broadly advertise planned aid deliveries through radio, megaphones, bulletins, or TV so that communities for which aid is intended can hold thieves accountable if they do not receive what they expect. Some agencies consciously lower the resale value of their aid goods without damaging their usefulness, thus undermining thieves' incentive. Others make theft so inconvenient that the effort required is not worth the return.

Strategies for delivering aid secretly thwart thieves' need for knowledge. Strategies for dispersing aid thwart both opportunity and incentive. Strategies for lowering the resale value of aid also undermine incentive. Strategies for informing and involving civilian communities in monitoring the distribution of aid address issues of impunity.

In the rest of this section we cite examples from a number of field sites. Although each of these strategies made sense in the place in which it was tried, no single approach can work everywhere. Aid workers must always consider the realities of their circumstances to come up with an effective approach that fits that setting. Chapter 6 presents an analytical framework to help aid workers consider the approaches that might work in their immediate situations. The examples given here provide rich background that can stimulate unconventional and imaginative ideas about what to do in other locations.

Not worth the effort.   In Somalia the Red Cross distributed blankets to families. Theft was common because blankets were scarce and profits could be made from their resale. Agency staff began to cut each blanket in half. Families could easily sew the blankets back together, but meanwhile their resale value dropped.

In other situations, aid agencies have stopped delivering high-priced grains and substituted sorghum or other less valuable but equally nourishing products. The food sustains recipients' health, but resale is not lucrative so there is little incentive for theft.

Making theft inconvenient.   An aid worker who has supervised many deliveries of grain and cooking oil to war victims reports that when shipments arrive, he routinely punches a hole in each bag of grain with his knife and removes the lids from the oil cans. Families can carry a bag of grain carefully, holding the hole closed to prevent spillage, and they can stuff straw into the opening of an oil can so it does not leak. But when thieves load cut bags into their trucks, much of the grain is lost as the bags bounce around. Oil cans piled in a truck slosh and spill and fi-

nally begin to slip and slide. The weight of shifting oil cans has occasionally caused trucks to tip over, losing everything.

Secrecy and dispersal.   In Cambodia one aid agency needed to take a
large amount of cash to an outlying field site to pay local staff. When
the cargo plane carrying the cash arrived at the airport, numerous
small vehicles met it. One bag of cash was loaded into the trunk of a
passenger car, two bags were tossed in the back of a truck, a jeep took
two, and a cart was loaded with one. Each carrier took a different route
to the office where the comptroller paid staff salaries as the money arrived. It was too difficult for thieves to locate and stop so many vehicles;
if they got one or two, the losses to the project were minimal. Thus the
gains to the thieves were not worth the effort.

Dispersal in a hurry.   In Tajikistan the United Nations High Commissioner for Refugees (UNHCR) imported housing materials communities needed to rebuild war-damaged homes. The materials were in great
demand. Local authorities, who had seized their positions in the recent
war, used their control of local rail and trucking to divert large amounts
of the material. Field staff knew that theft usually occurred at night and
that a few watchmen would be powerless against the gangs of thieves.
They organized a massive and immediate distribution of the materials
on the day they arrived by train, ensuring that they were in the recipient
communities by nightfall. Once in the communities, the building supplies were better protected. The dispersal of goods to those who would
use them reduced the opportunity for thieves and heightened the communities' ability to hold thieves accountable.

Identifying thieves.   In a West African country, one agency was helping
women with public health issues. As part of this program, the agency distributed inexpensive radios to the village women so they could listen to a
weekly series on rebuilding civil society. Soon all of the radios had been
stolen. The agency staff reissued radios—this time painted bright pink.
Any man seen with a pink radio was immediately accosted and challenged by others. No one could easily get away with stealing the radios.

Civilian protectors.   In Chechnya aid agency vehicles traveling between
communities were often the objects of theft; sometimes they were
stolen themselves, sometimes aid workers in the trucks were taken
hostage (for later ransom demands), and sometimes cash, computers,
or other valuables were stolen. Drivers were told not to pick up hitch-
hikers. Some realized, however, that if they offered rides to elderly men

from the local communities and sat them prominently in the front of the truck, car jackings were less likely to occur because any action against a vehicle in which a respected elder was riding would be considered a hostile act by his clan, and reprisals would follow. The theft of aid goods would be associated with the disruption of interclan relations, which were closely guarded and controlled by elder councils. The costs of theft thus became too high to make it worthwhile.

Glut the market.   In Afghanistan a World Food Programme (WFP) staff person told of distributing seeds within the volatile circumstances of local, intergroup fighting. During the first year one group could control the seeds, but after that farmers propagated, sold, and traded seeds; thus seed values fell, and everyone had access to seed.

In other circumstances aid agencies have imported enough goods to glut the market; resale value for thieves thus becomes marginal. A caution: These goods must not compete with locally produced goods or they will undermine local production and increase dependence on outside aid. This strategy should be used only when goods cannot be produced at the recipient site.

Other not-so-good options.   Some options to avoid theft have later been found to have a negative impact; they include hiring armed guards to ride with convoys or to protect warehouses, threatening to pull aid programs out of a region if goods are stolen, and hiring local merchants to manage delivery. These methods are discussed later, but we should note here that in some cases hiring armed guards and threatening to withdraw aid programs can reinforce a war culture, and hiring local merchants can reinforce a war economy by making the continuation of aid (and hence of the war that prompts it) profitable.

Aid Affects Markets

Wars distort economies. Patterns of production, employment, trade, and services shift to war-related activities and patterns. Some people are enriched by war, whereas many are impoverished. Some trade linkages are supported, but others are disrupted.

Aid can reinforce market distortions by feeding the war economy and undermining peacetime production and productivity. For example, when aid agencies hire guards from local militias to protect their goods and their staff, those payments directly reinforce economic systems of conflict. When aid agencies import goods that can be produced

> In Bosnia and Herzegovina, immediately after the Dayton Peace Agreement, drivers who had crisscrossed the country to deliver food and supplies to civilians under fire talked of their uncertainties once the convoys stopped. Which of them would be retained as drivers of the reduced number of NGO vehicles? How could they use their wartime experience to find peacetime jobs? One driver said, "Driving the aid convoys during the war was dangerous, but this seems like nothing next to the dangers of peace. Not only my immediate family but also my grandparents, aunts, uncles, and cousins depend on my income. I almost dread this peace and wish for war again."

locally and distribute them at no cost, they can undermine peacetime economic incentives.

Aid often creates its own "industries" in recipient countries in which profits can be made and wages can be paid. Because of the wealth aid represents and the systems it relies on, profits can be made by local people who control the assets aid needs. War disrupts distribution systems and routes, which aid agencies need to reach at-risk populations. Individuals and groups that control delivery and access can gain both financially and politically.

Demand for other assets also rises when aid agencies arrive. The costs of hotel rooms, office space, housing, food, furniture, and equipment are bid up by the influx of expatriates. People who own or control these facilities and goods can become wealthy in the midst of the otherwise deteriorating economic conditions associated with war.

Aid creates jobs and pays wages. Aid agencies hire local people who speak the languages of the aid staff; they also hire drivers, housekeepers, guards, gardeners, and warehousers. If the demand for limited skills is sufficient, wages can be significantly inflated by the presence of international employers. (Often, as discussed later, this has a further distributional effect that increases tensions among groups at war.)

Whenever local individuals or groups gain economically from the presence of aid—whether because they are hired as translators, drivers, or managers or because they own needed hotels, houses, or vehicles—the influx of massive aid can reinforce their interest in perpetuating the war economy. When an economy is so thoroughly disrupted by war that few nonwar economic opportunities exist, the people whose economic survival is linked to war-related enterprises (including, alas, aid) develop a stake in the continuation of the conflict. If peace is expected to lead to a rapid cessation of aid (rather than to a transition to a situation

of development assistance), individuals and their families whose livelihoods come through aid are seriously threatened. When profits made
by servicing the aid community are high, incentives are correspondingly high. And when the goods and services the aid agencies buy, rent,
or hire are connected to warring militias, the conflict-reinforcing
process can become virtually a closed circuit.

Aid can also affect trading patterns that link people. If aid organizations import goods that were previously supplied by one group to another and those two groups are in conflict, aid reinforces the new division.

What to Do: Programming Options

Few aid agencies assess either the local capacity to supply the goods
they need or the impact of their local purchases on war profiteering. To
avoid reinforcing the war economy and undermining the peace economy, they should do so. But this seems a daunting and complicated cal-
culation, especially under the pressures of an emergency situation.

NGOs, however, often operate in delineated areas. Under these
conditions, it is not difficult to assess rather accurately supply and demand for the goods and services used and provided by aid. Even in a
larger area (as when an NGO has programs across an entire country),
agency staff usually know what is available and how prices are affected
by aid's demands and imported resources.

The more difficult problem is how to adjust programming approaches on the basis of what is known about price effects. This is especially difficult for field staff when donor policies and aid agency headquarters push deliveries of imported aid goods, as they often do.

What does NGO experience show? First, to avoid undermining
peacetime economic activity, some agencies buy aid goods locally rather
than import them. When these purchases are focused on the support of
normal peacetime economic activities (such as agriculture) rather than
on special war-related enterprises (such as guard services for goods
transported across warring lines), they can help to maintain and reinforce peacetime systems and institutions.

Second, to avoid bidding up prices in ways that reinforce incentives
for the continuation of aid (and war), agencies have sometimes agreed
to fixed price and wage rates for local goods and services. If they peg
these rates at reasonable levels that resemble peacetime prices, the transition to a peacetime economy can be eased by preserving indigenous
productive capacity and not reinforcing incentives for wartime profits.
(As we discuss in Chapter 5, however, keeping local hires' wages and
salaries low can convey an unintended message that local people are

In Somalia, one agency planned and negotiated its aid program in the market square on market days where everyone could hear and be a part of the discussions. When offering to provide funds to rebuild destroyed community buildings, the agency's staff announced exactly how much money was available to each community. Crowds that gathered in the market talked about what they needed, debated community priorities, and, with much discussion, agreed on what should happen and how much it should cost. When a local carpenter or roofer was asked to give an estimate for his work on a project, he would often see this as an opportunity to profit from aid. Hearing his price, his neighbors would hoot and laugh: "No! That's too high. You built another building just last month for a lot less." Public scrutiny reduced opportunism, ensured fair valuation of work, and also ensured the completion and quality of the work. When it was time to pay the workers, the agency did so in full view of the entire community in the public market where the original negotiations had been carried out.

less valued than international staff. Some of the programming ideas described later attempt to address these two issues by balancing reasonable wage rates with other benefits such as training and loans.)

In part because of donor and headquarters policies that push aid imports and in part because field staff have not done in situ assessments of supply and demand for the products and services they use and deliver, examples of agency experiences in successfully avoiding negative market impacts are scarce. Discussions with field staff in a variety of places, however, have produced some approaches that might work.

1. When NGOs hire local people during crisis situations, they could include training for what could become peacetime employment. Aid agencies could reinforce such training programs by providing small-scale loans to help their local staff set up new enterprises during the transition from war to peace.

2. Aid agencies could establish wage rates for local staff that during war would represent a decent (not a war-profit) rate. In addition, they could guarantee a lump-sum payment upon their departure or a "bonus" payment if peace is declared. Again, locally hired staff would be expected to use such payments to form peacetime enterprises.

3. Individuals' ability to make unwarranted profits because of war conditions often involves an element of secrecy and threat. If decisions regarding payments are located in a broad community base, individuals may be held accountable, and their incentives and opportunities to

make unreasonable incomes from war may be limited. War profiteering may be best controlled by community accountability.

4. Finally, people in war societies have often expressed dismay when they realize that they have become economically dependent on aid. Most people strongly prefer to be independent. Aid agencies can encourage and support this preference by discussing it with their local staff and with aid recipients. Aid agencies have more experience than local people in understanding the ways wars distort economies and the difficulties of a transition to peace. Thus initiating such discussions may help people plan how they can best make the transition to peace.

Distributional Impacts

Differential benefits from aid can reinforce intergroup tensions in conflict areas. When aid is targeted toward some groups and others are excluded, competition between them is fueled. When returning refugees receive aid and people who stayed in a war zone during the fighting receive none, tensions can result. When aid agencies label people according to their needs and focus assistance programs accordingly, they can reinforce subgroup identities and accentuate intergroup differences.

Aid agencies target subgroups for good reasons. With limited resources, they must set priorities and focus on where the need is greatest. They often direct aid toward people who have been marginalized or impoverished by their own societies. Furthermore, aid staff know that when aid is given without regard for group differences, people with power can use it for their own ends and further disadvantage those without power, which is why NGOs make gender and vulnerability analyses an integral part of aid planning. Nonetheless, experience shows that in conflict settings targeting aid reinforces divisions rather than connectors in societies.

When an aid agency initiated a program of postwar housing reconstruction in Tajikistan, it targeted its program toward those who had suffered the most damage. This group, the Garmi, had also lost the war. (This is often the case—i.e., that aid assistance focused on those who suffered the most will most often reach those who lost the conflict.) The Kulyabi who had won resented the fact that the international aid community was restrengthening the "enemy" whom they had defeated. They saw this as a political rather than a humanitarian act.

When Hutu communities fled into eastern Zaire from Rwanda after their militias had committed genocide against their Tutsi and moderate Hutu neighbors, they arrived in a stark, inhospitable land where survival was unlikely. The international community responded with humanitarian aid to avoid the catastrophe of cholera, hunger, and death that surely would have ensued. Very little aid went to Rwanda where those who had survived the genocide were also at risk because of war-induced damage, food shortages, and psychological trauma. The fact that international aid was directed more toward those who had committed genocide and toward the communities that accompanied them in their flight than toward the people who had suffered from the genocide continues to disturb both Rwandans and aid workers.

In subsequent months aid agencies tried to correct this bias by focusing assistance inside Rwanda on "genocide survivors." Some Rwandans have again challenged this targeting, noting that every label emphasizes differences (and results in differential benefits from aid) rather than commonness. They propose that aid be labeled *community based*, available to everyone in a given area in which needs are shared by different groups.

Aid's profit and wage effects can also reinforce intergroup tensions. Ownership of the assets aid agencies need is often differentially distributed among local groups; thus the profits to be gained from aid are also unevenly distributed. When aid agencies hire local people who can speak their language, such benefits can be biased because foreign language ability (and other skills needed by aid agencies) is often related to educational access that, in turn, is correlated with patterns of privilege and discrimination. Uneven benefits from aid, if realized according to subgroup identities, can exacerbate tensions between groups.

What to Do: Programming Options

To avoid exacerbating tensions between groups, aid workers have organized programs in which for anyone to gain, everyone must gain. They have used aid to reinforce people's shared interests. They have developed committees or relied on existing leadership structures (such as the religious leaders) in which responsibility for distributional decisions is publicly discussed and decided. When people are involved in decisions about how to distribute aid, they often understand and accept distributions that favor the most needy even though they are from another group.

In Tajikistan, when the war ended in Khatlon Province and Kulyabi and Garmi villages were returning to normal, international NGOs were eager to help villages establish enterprises to replace the jobs and income they had lost when the cotton industry collapsed. Realizing that the two groups had just gone through the damaging experience of a civil war, some NGOs assumed they would not be ready to work together in common enterprises. Those NGOs developed strategies to help each monoethnic village become economically self-reliant.

Recognizing that for many years Garmis and Kulyabis had worked side by side on the state farms, one NGO designed its aid program to reemphasize that history of economic interaction and interdependence. In a Garmi village the NGO supported the development of a wool-production enterprise, and in a nearby Kulyabi village it supported traditional rug weaving. Although the two groups did not work in the same space, they readily agreed that the wool producers would supply raw materials for the rug producers. Each enterprise depended on the success of the other for its own success.

We noted earlier that markets can be connectors. We discussed how aid interacts with wartime and peacetime economies, how its purchases and imports affect prices and wages, and how prices and wages affect the incentives and possibilities for continuing war or moving toward peace.

Here we are making an additional point: namely, that aid's resources can be directed toward linking people's interests and enlarging or reinforcing their interdependence. They can provide incentives for

In Bosnia and Herzegovina an NGO that delivered aid to Gorazde had to pass through the Republic of Srbska to reach the distribution area. Each time a convoy drove this route, Serb villagers threw stones at the trucks. Agency staff understood the anger of the bypassed groups even though their need for outside aid was minimal. They met with leaders in the bypassed villages and negotiated to buy the goods needed in Gorazde from those villages if they could supply them. When the convoys began to carry locally produced goods to the people on the other side, they met no resistance. The external agency arranged a trade between those who could supply goods and those who needed them that war-induced divisions kept the two sides from arranging for themselves. Everyone benefited.

When the war ended in Lebanon, both government and aid agencies were contracting local engineering and construction firms to carry out massive rebuilding of war-damaged areas. These companies were often owned and run by families directly aligned with one of the factions that had been at war. In the postwar period, every contract thus became a focus of interfactional competition. To alleviate this problem, some people suggested that aid agencies should stipulate that preference would be given to contractors who demonstrated that they had hired people from different factional groups to work together.

In postwar Cambodia, when refugees returned from the Thai camps to villages in which resources were already severely strained, everyone knew tensions would be high between returnees and local people who had stayed in Cambodia during the war. As UNHCR initiated its program of Quick Impact Projects, through which it provided funds to villages to facilitate the absorption of returnees, someone suggested that the group should add a component to address potential tensions between the groups. As UNHCR provided funds for digging wells, clearing land, or rebuilding community structures, it could give priority to applications from villages in which returnees and "stayees" had jointly developed proposals.

people to work together on nonwar activities and issues and can create space for people who wish to act in nonwar ways.

Substitution Effects of Aid

In some circumstances external aid can fill so great a proportion of civilian needs for food, shelter, safety, and health services that significant local resources are thereby freed up for the pursuit of war. This economic substitution effect of aid has a further political impact. When external aid agencies assume responsibility for civilian survival, warlords tend to define their responsibility and accountability only in terms of military control. Even if they started with a commitment to peacetime political leadership, as the international aid community takes over the tasks of feeding and providing health services and shelter for civilians these military-oriented leaders increasingly relinquish responsibility for civilian welfare. They focus on military ends and, over time, define their roles solely in terms of physical control (and the violent at-tainment and maintenance of that control). As this occurs, warriors struggling for victory over space and people lose all interest and com-petence in civilian affairs and become increasingly ill prepared to as-sume broad, responsible leadership in a postwar period.

What to Do: Programming Options

To avoid the economic substitution effects that free up local resources for the pursuit of war, some aid agencies limit inputs to minimal levels. Rather than supply resources for civilians from the outside, they focus on ways to support local efforts to meet local needs that reinforce peacetime economic activities.

The political side effect of the substitution effect poses another challenge. In the next section, after we discuss how aid legitimizes peo-ple and actions, we describe ways aid agency staff can promote rather than substitute for commanders' nonwar actions.

Aid Legitimizes People and Actions

Aid can reinforce the power of warriors to wage war by adding to their resource base through either theft or the substitution effect discussed earlier. Even more common and significant, however, is the fact that aid agencies, operating in areas controlled by factions, must often make "le-gitimate" payments to those in power in the form of taxes or fees for services (import-export licenses, hired guards for protection, loaned use of vehicles, and the like).

When they control a given geographic area, commanders have the right to expect that external aid agencies will comply with the rules and restrictions they impose in their area of command. They may tax aid goods, impose duties, establish currency exchange rates, and restrict delivery sites and times because they are acting in a role of governance. They can use that income to finance the war or to enrich themselves. They can use aid delivery sites to control where people can (or cannot) live and thus control their loyalties or force their removal from areas.

Further, when aid agencies need the permission of armed factions to gain access to people with whom they must work, that situation rein-forces factional power and legitimacy. Some aid staff working in south-ern Sudan report that Operation Lifeline Sudan (OLS)—a system for negotiation established by aid agencies to ensure equal and unimpeded access to all civilian populations—has become a "legitimating" force in that region. Aspiring commanders have sometimes used negotiations with OLS to gain approval as legitimate wielders of power over certain populations or regions.

When aid agencies have tried to avoid dealing with the armed factions that control the areas in which they work, they have experienced direct and sometimes dire consequences. They have become targets for theft and threats, and the intended aid recipients have sometimes been attacked.

These are the contextual political realities that circumscribe aid's pursuit of humanitarian goals. The constraints are serious. We have asked aid workers in many war zones how they avoid interacting with and legitimizing warriors. In each case we have been told "it is impossible to avoid them."

"But," aid workers say, "the real issue is *how* to interact with warriors." What can aid providers do?

What to Do: Programming Options

First, let us consider what does not work. Often, to avoid giving warlords legitimacy aid personnel approach their interactions with reluctance or hostility. This tends to set up an antagonistic relationship, which aid personnel see as demonstrating that they do not agree with or condone the actions of the person in power. As will be discussed more fully in Chapter 5, however, such approaches tend to reinforce, or at least excuse in their eyes, the very actions of the warlords that aid workers decry.

We noted earlier that warriors will try to use the resources or power in their areas in their pursuit of victory and control. But benign rulers also use available resources to buttress their governance. To understand how aid workers can avoid reinforcing illegitimate power, we must analyze what is illegitimate about that power.

We do not want to support oppression inflicted through violence and threat. We do not want to legitimate self-serving power and greed. Furthermore, we should not want to take responsibility for governance—or to presume that we know the appropriate systems of governance for the people with whom we work. That is their job, not ours.

We do want to support the ability of communities to hold their leaders accountable for civilian welfare. We do want to provide support for people to act and think in nonwar, rather than warlike, ways. We want to leave behind a civil society that has been strengthened rather than weakened by its interactions with aid.

From this perspective the question becomes not how to avoid warlords but how to encourage (push?) them to assume responsibility for civilian welfare and reduce their thuggery. Efforts to affect such changes do not produce immediate transformations. Although experi-

The commander in my area is a scoundrel and a murderer. When I first came to the area, I had to go see him to negotiate access to the villages where we work. At first he tried to put me off, but I arrived early one morning when I knew he was in his headquarters and barged in. I told him in no uncertain terms, "We are here to give aid to the people who are suffering in your region. They need it and you know it. We've got major aid, but believe me we're not letting you or your thugs near it! Now these are the terms on which we will work here—no interference of any kind from you or your soldiers. If any of your guys so much as tries to stop us at a roadblock, we're out of here."

Well, he knew I meant what I said, so he agreed. Of course, he pretended he cared about the people, too, but I know he only robs them. Anyway, so far we've had only one incident. One of his henchmen who was raging drunk shook his rifle in the face of one of our drivers at a checkpoint. I was steamed! I stormed into the commander's office and shouted that if he couldn't control his thugs any better than that, we were gone. I demanded an apology. Of course, he would not apologize, but he did say he'd look into it, and we know he disciplined that soldier a few days later. These guys only understand power. They'll really take advantage of you if you're not tough.

—Aid workers in Liberia, Afghanistan, southern Sudan, Somalia, and other regions had similar stories

ence is limited, some programming approaches have been tried with good effects.

1. To lower the probability that warlords will use aid in pursuit of greed, agencies have limited the supplies they import and have designed them to have value for use but not for sale (as discussed previously in the section on theft).

2. To lower the levels of threat and coercion that characterize conflict situations, some aid agencies have consciously not used aid resources to threaten, bribe, or coerce compliance with their programs. They have set a different tone in their interactions with warlords that emphasizes and demonstrates tolerance, respect, trust, and commitment. To do this without naïveté is tricky. In Chapter 5 we discuss in more detail possibilities for and experiences with providing aid in war zones with an alternative tone.

3. To co-opt commanders into assuming responsibility for civilian welfare, aid agencies have established systems that presume commander concern for welfare and reinforce commanders' involvement in

bettering people's lives. For example, they have set up regular meetings with commanders or their representatives to discuss all aspects of aid to civilians, they have taken authorities to visit project sites to interact with people there, and they have exposed commanders to the real impacts their policies have on people's lives. Some examples follow.

In Liberia one agency field director had to deal with a particularly unsavory commander. Rather than avoid him or demand his compliance with humanitarian aid terms, the director made an appointment with the commander and explained quietly why humanitarian assistance matters, as well as his own and his agency's commitment to help suffering people. He sought "permission" to work in the area, and it was granted. He asked for regular appointments with the commander "so we can keep you abreast of what we are doing," and the commander agreed. Over the weeks the commander—once thought to be a thug—began to ask about people's needs: "How do you know malnutrition is a problem? How do you know what the people want?" As the aid staff explained their methods of working with people, the commander, who had previously had an interest in control only through arms, began to accept responsibility for civilian welfare. He ultimately went to the villages with the aid director to "see for himself," and he began to adopt more effective policies. Although this story is unusual both in the approach taken by the aid person and in the response evoked from the commander, it suggests that under some circumstances aid workers can experiment with different approaches and possibly support positive changes.

In Tajikistan the government in Dushanbe adopted postwar policies prejudicial to the area of Khatlon Province in which much of the fighting had occurred. The government defended the policies by citing information about the situation in the province that the agencies working there knew was incorrect. The director of a lead agency reported that after he had invited some ministers to accompany him to Khatlon, some central policies were adjusted to benefit people in the hinterland.

These are some of the ways aid resources feed into war or can avoid doing so and, in some cases, support local capacities for peace. In Chapter 5 we examine how aid's implicit ethical messages interact with conflict.

5

Aid's Impact on Conflict Through Implicit Ethical Messages

In addition to delivering goods and services, aid delivers messages. The content, style, and modes of aid communicate values, which can also reinforce, prolong, and exacerbate conflict or reinforce and support capacities for peace. The messages of aid are linked to and interact with the impacts of aid's resources discussed in Chapter 4.

The explicit and recognized message of aid is ethical and important: that all innocent civilians caught in warfare on any side of a conflict should as a matter of principle have access to assistance. Furthermore, in our imperfect world, where suffering is imposed on people through no fault of their own, others must be able to reach out to them with spiritual and physical succor. We cannot accept a world in which receiving or giving aid is restricted or thwarted.

Many aid providers believe these explicit messages are so clear that they are always understood by aid recipients and others in society. Unfortunately, because aid also conveys implicit messages often unrecognized by providers, the messages many recipients receive are ambiguous. Some of the dilemmas aid workers face are better understood when these implicit messages are clarified.

We have identified seven implicit ethical messages of humanitarian and development aid in conflict settings that negatively reinforce the war environment. First we describe them and illustrate how they work. We then discuss their implications for the ways in which aid is designed, managed, and delivered.

Implicit Ethical Messages of Aid That Reinforce Conflict

Arms and Power

When aid agencies hire armed guards to protect their goods from theft and their workers from harm, the implicit message received by those in the war zone is that it is legitimate for arms to determine who gains access to food and medical supplies and that security and safety are derived from weapons. This, of course, is how warlords also understand arms. They believe that through might they have a right to control people's access to goods and to political participation. They believe that to be secure, one must have more firepower than anyone else.

Aid agencies protest, "Our aims are worthy; when we employ guards, the weapons support good ends." Every warlord will make the same claim.

It is impossible for aid to adopt the modes of warfare without reinforcing their legitimacy. The implicit ethical message of the use of arms reinforces the belligerence and reliance on threat to achieve goals that pervade the war environment.

Disrespect, Mistrust, and Competition Among Aid Agencies

Another negative implicit ethical message is conveyed by the failure of aid agencies to cooperate with each other. Aid agency field workers report that they often bad-mouth other agencies' work. They compete for aid recipients, often by criticizing the program approaches of other agencies and refusing to have anything to do with them. Sometimes this situation results from a fundamental difference in outlook (as when some agencies take an explicit religious stance and others decry proselytizing); sometimes it results from personality clashes among field-based staff; sometimes it reflects different politics, either that of the donor country from which the aid agencies come or politics in relation to the events occurring in the recipient country.

The message conveyed to people in a recipient community is that it is unnecessary to cooperate with people they do not like; our work has no space for tolerance of differences, and we do not and need not respect people with whom we disagree. These attitudes permeate and underlie the intergroup conflicts that shape the space within which aid is provided.

Aid Workers and Impunity

Aid workers function under difficult and sometimes dangerous circumstances. They have few outlets for recreation. The pressures of their work can lead to physical exhaustion and emotional burnout. To maintain psychological and physical health, they must find ways to relax and even to enjoy themselves. For example, aid workers may take agency vehicles for a weekend excursion to the mountains even though gasoline

In a situation in which a tremendous and sudden influx of refugees occurred, conditions for aid workers were extremely stressed. They faced daily threats from militia members who lived in the camps. They worked long hours and still could not keep up with the growing need for medical attention, food, and shelter as refugees poured into the area. They were stricken by the people's suffering before they arrived in the camps; they were drained by the constant tales of horrors experienced and suffering endured.

The field director knew his staff members were pushed. They lived together in a large house with a garden where they could be safe at night, but he could not allow them to leave the area once darkness came. The house had a swimming pool but no water. Knowing that the water trucks passed nearby each day on their way to the camps and knowing there was plenty of water so no one would die from lack of it, the director diverted one of the trucks to his staff compound to fill the swimming pool so his staff could have a chance to relax each evening after work. They could thus maintain their energy and spirits even in the difficult working conditions.

An aid worker recounted that he and his fellow staff had worked very hard in an emergency situation. He remembered the stress they felt from the constant pressure of jobs to be done. When he returned home and had his film developed, however, he noted how many pictures showed him and his colleagues enjoying a large meal together, leaning on their cars drinking beer, or lounging under a tree with food or drink. He was both amused and amazed. He concluded that the atmosphere of constant pressure was in part a mind-set rather than a full reality. He declared that he would never again claim there was "no time" to think, discuss, plan, and consider options.

---

supplies are low and prices are high. They may have parties in the aid compound with beer, music, and good food even though the people they are there to assist have little food or joy.

When aid workers use their goods and support systems for their own pleasure, local people who have few or no resources and depend on those of the aid system see this behavior as acting with impunity. The message is that if one has control over resources, one can use them for personal purposes and pleasure. Accountability is unnecessary.

Warlords use the resources they control in this way. They use them for personal pleasure and to reward cronies.

Different Values for Different Lives

Working in dangerous settings (and even in ones that are not so dangerous), aid agencies adopt policies that apply differently to expatriate and local staffs. Salary levels are set at widely divergent rates. Vehicles are signed out to expatriate staff or drivers are sent to pick them up, whereas local people are expected to use local transportation or to walk. Radios are given to expatriate staff but rarely to local staff.

Plans for staff evacuation in the event of sudden danger often focus on expatriate staff, vehicles, and communications equipment and assume that local people can manage for themselves. When evacuations occur, aid workers report that food, medicines, and local staff are often left behind, whereas expatriate personnel with vehicles, radios, and other office equipment are rescued.

The implicit ethical message is one of inequality. It is a message of a differential value of lives (expatriate over local) and even of time (expatriate staff deserve rides, whereas local staff must take several hours to walk to work each day). Even worse is the message that imported goods have a higher value than the lives of local people (radio equipment is evacuated but not local staff).

In conflict settings, many value distinctions are made between groups. "We" deserve safety, comfort, and convenience but have no responsibility for seeing that "they" have those things.

Powerlessness

Field-based aid staff often assert their powerlessness over events around them: "I can't do anything to change this. It is the fault of my headquarters (or the donors or the local people or the evil warlords). Because I am not in charge and cannot control everything that affects me, I am not responsible for the impact of my limited actions."

The implicit message of powerlessness and thus of nonresponsibility for the effects of one's actions is clear. If aid workers, with all of their resources and apparent power, feel unable to change things or that they are not responsibe for the impacts of their choices, then no one need feel differently.

In all conflict areas local people express their powerlessness in relation to greater forces. For many, it is someone else's job to change things, to take responsibility, to improve the situation, to make peace.

Bad actions are explained as the fault of someone else's decision, order, or pressure.

Belligerence, Tension, Suspicion

When aid workers are nervous about conflict and concerned for their own safety, they often act in ways that increase tension and suspicion. Such actions can also heighten the likelihood of a violent incident. Field staff tell of their apprehension as they approach checkpoints manned by soldiers. One reaction is to be assertive and belligerent, to expect the worst and assume a defensive posture against it: "You have no right to stop this truck. Don't you see the name of our aid agency on our door? You must let me pass."

One message is "I have the power here, not you." In a war environment, this is both a provocative message and one that reinforces the atmosphere and modes of interaction prevalent among contesting groups.

Another message is "You are mean and untrustworthy. I know you only understand toughness. I'm interacting with you in the only way you'll understand." This message limits the range of possible and likely human interaction by assuming the worst in others. It can reinforce the likelihood that the worst will happen.

Publicity

One implicit message is conveyed by NGO headquarters' policies and approaches to publicity and fund-raising. When aid agencies use gruesome pictures of war or cite acute suffering from atrocities in an effort to elicit public sympathy and funds, they can reinforce the demonization of one side in a war. Further, some evidence (although it is difficult to pin down) indicates that unscrupulous fighters have occasionally committed atrocities against their own people to play to the international sentiments stirred up by such publicity pieces.

Implications for Aid: Programming Options

Do these seven implicit ethical messages imply that the best aid worker is one who is unarmed at all times; who works collaboratively with all other aid workers regardless of differences in principle or approach; who lives unostentatiously and never relaxes to identify fully with aid recipients; who is last in line for vehicles, radios, and evacuation in case of a crisis; who feels and asserts his or her efficacy in everyday work in spite of the odds against having any influence; who always believes the best about everyone despite all evidence to the contrary; and who works for the ideal agency that never stoops to use sad-eyed children in its advertising? Is this the profile of an aid worker that we propose for the future?

Such a profile is, of course, unrealistic. And in all likelihood the aid worker described would not survive for long. In the real world of wars—where many people are acting from extremely selfish interests, wielding power through weaponry, acting with impunity, and caring little or nothing about the value of human life—how can aid agency staff members work without reinforcing the moods and modes of war? What options do they have that guarantee a degree of safety in these conditions?

The implicit messages noted in the previous section involve attitudes and approaches, lifestyles, and the safety of aid workers. We examine each of these and its implications for aid policies and field-level programming. Again, we look to past aid experience to discover realistic options for avoiding negative impacts and establishing an alternative nonwar mode of operating.

Attitudes

Some cynics claim aid is an "industry" that "uses" the suffering of others to guarantee agency survival and that staff members are mere functionaries of this industry whose employment depends on crises. If such agencies and individuals exist, they are rare. In our experience, the vast majority of aid workers are motivated by a sincere wish to help.

Circumstances, however, alter attitudes. When aid workers are cheated, disrespected, or threatened, an adversarial element creeps into the aid giver–aid recipient relationship. When they are exhausted and see no immediate effects from their labors, aid workers lose sight of ways they may affect positive change. When they work with suffering people day after day and under constant tension, they toughen up and develop an ability to distance themselves from those they help. When the context is one of conflict, the atmosphere of tension, belligerence, and mistrust can be contagious.

But experience shows that aid workers, mindful of the potential impact of their attitudes on local people, can take small (and sometimes large) actions that can make a major difference. A few examples follow. Each illustrates how the attitudes of aid workers directly affect their routine actions in their work. They also suggest how powerful even simple actions can be.

The Taliban arrived in Herat and issued a ruling that women could no longer work in the public sphere. This ruling affected the Afghan women who had been hired by NGOs to work with other women in the society.

A former mujahidin who worked with one of the international NGOs that had an active program in Herat was worried. He knew that because men cannot work directly with women, the Taliban ruling seriously threatened his agency's women's programs. So he visited the Taliban headquarters to discuss the issue.

"I went over one night," he reported, "and we sat and drank tea and talked for a long time. I explained why it is so important for our female staff members to continue to work. But when I finished, the Taliban commander said 'no.'"

He smiled as he recounted the story. "I went home discouraged, but then I realized that I must not have explained the issues well enough. I know those guys are smart, and I know they care about their mothers and wives and daughters. So I went back again." He reported that he "failed to explain it well enough" on four other occasions, but finally, when he tried the fifth time, the Taliban commander "understood and agreed."

Later Taliban policies reversed this "understanding and agreement" and foreclosed all opportunities for women to work. This story is challenging because it raises the question of whose fault it is if aid staff do not get their ideas across to warriors and how many times they should try.

A young and inexperienced aid worker was heading off to Somalia when things were still insecure in many parts of the country. He telephoned his father to say goodbye and asked if he had any advice. His father replied, "Just keep smiling."

That was, he says, "the most important advice I received." Many times, when approaching a hostile-looking group of frightened soldiers at a roadblock, he remembered his father's words and assumed a posture of friendly openness. This not only made him feel better and more confident but also seemed to evoke calmer, sometimes even friendly responses. He used the advice again when his aid agency sent him to begin programs in Rwanda while the genocide was still under way. "I found that people responded," he says. "They seemed surprised and relieved that I would act as if I trusted them."

In an LCPP feedback workshop in Sarajevo, one aid worker looked up with a rueful smile. "Every time I relax with my local staff," she said, "I ask them to tell me about their war experiences. The more horrible the story, the more riveted my attention. I commiserate, and together we relive the horrors of the war."

She continued, "What if I asked them instead to tell me about their relationships with the 'other side' before the war? What if we spent more time talking about people they like and trust from the other side? What if we dealt with what they would like their future to be?

"I just realized that I am reinforcing their negative experiences and attitudes with my questions. I seem more interested in how bad things are than in how to improve them. What kind of example am I setting?"

Lifestyle Issues

Aid workers live in difficult circumstances. Separation from family, potential danger, and surrounding tension are difficult to live with day after day. Aid recipients live in difficult circumstances. Separation from family, potential danger, and surrounding tension are difficult to live with day after day.

The two groups should be closely bound by their common experience. In most aid settings they are not.

One essential difference cannot be ignored. Aid workers are present in the difficult circumstances by their own choice and are free to leave, also by their own choice. Aid recipients are present because they have no other option. If they could leave, most would do so.

Other differences between the two groups are created by the ways aid workers live in relation to aid recipients. The lifestyle choices of aid agency staff can undermine their working relationships with the people they intend to help. These choices can differentiate, alienate, and antagonize recipients and set in motion the attitudes and processes by which aid providers and recipients become locked into a mutual mistrust. Too often, aid processes lead to a situation in which recipients try to "get everything we can" and providers "have to control everything because we can't trust these people."

Increasingly, aid agency staff are discussing the dilemmas posed by their need to live in a way that allows them to maintain physical and mental health and to do their work and at the same time does not separate them so fully from the people around them. Simple things seem to help. One aid worker learns the names of the children of local staff members and aid recipients with whom he works. He talks about his own children and shows people their pictures. Another worker makes it a point never to seem to be in a rush. She consciously takes time to sit down and look at the people with whom she is talking. She tries to remember to listen—really—to what they are telling her and to give a genuine rather than an automatic response. She says doing this takes no more time than rushing.

In one postwar setting, the aid agency staff compound served as a center for open discussion. At a given hour each day, the project director was available (with tea and coffee served) to hear anyone's problem or to discuss any issue with visitors. Local committees would visit with requests. People stopped by out of curiosity or for pleasure. People from all sides of the earlier war were welcome.

Some agency staff choose to live with the people they are helping. They take public transportation, learn the local language, and live simply. They make friends among recipients, sharing meals and going to weddings, baptisms, circumcisions, and other local ceremonies. They shop in local shops and eat what local people eat.

But many aid agencies limit the choices their staff can make about where and how to live in a conflict setting. The agencies assume responsibility for safety; hence, they develop systems for protection that often involve separation from local people.

Safety

Lifestyle issues are closely related to safety issues. Increasingly, aid workers are subject to threats of kidnapping and even murder. In late 1996 aid workers were killed or detained in Chechnya, Rwanda, Sudan, Afghanistan, and Tajikistan. The incidence of violence against humanitarian aid staff has increased sharply in recent years and in recent conflicts.[1]

Recent attempts to enlist military protection for aid workers has largely failed to reduce these threats, in part because donor governments have been reluctant to assign troops to some current conflict areas. But even when they have done so, the security of aid personnel has not improved. On the contrary, some evidence indicates that as foreign troops have moved into conflict settings to protect aid workers with arms, they have provoked hostility among local warring factions that see those forces as another contender for power. Although aid workers may be safer when traveling in convoys with international protection, this temporary show of force may provoke resentment that actually increases overall dangers. In a war setting, military might (even when used for "good" reasons) seems to provoke a response.

> When the humanitarian agency staff members left their hotel in downtown Beirut for their appointments each day, they told their taxi driver where they wanted to go. Many days, they reported, the driver would say: "No, not today. Perhaps you would just as soon go to 'x' quarter of the city today?"
>
> They always took the driver's advice. Inevitably, they would learn that at some time during the day a localized battle had taken place in the area where they had originally asked to go.

Some of the increased danger humanitarian workers face is derived from the generalized lawlessness that prevails in many areas of recent conflict. This heightened danger has also been associated with a breakdown in both regulated warfare, fought according to international rules, and acceptance of and adherence to international humanitarian principles.

Additionally, more aid workers are found in almost all current conflict settings than were present even a decade ago (with the possible exception of the cross-border operations in which a large number of international aid agencies provided aid from Pakistan to Afghanistan). Furthermore, the quantity and value of goods distributed through the nongovernmental aid sector have increased dramatically. Although it is impossible to assign causation, at least some of the new dangers encountered by aid agency personnel seem to result from these two changes. As the number of NGOs operating in any crisis has increased, there are more aid workers, and they become easier targets. As the quantity and value of aid goods have increased, the value of aid to warriors has also increased. Theft and kidnapping become increasingly worthwhile as the potential wealth to be realized increases. Further, when aid appears to be a big business, with many actors and numerous valuable goods, it takes on the characteristics of an anonymous big actor and thus becomes a target for hostility.

In Chapter 4 we cited many creative ways in which aid staff have avoided the theft of aid resources without relying on armed guards and the threat of weaponry. We have few examples of ways that aid agencies have ensured the safety of their staff without relying on guards, radio communications, and militarily backed evacuation plans.

Experience seems to suggest, however, that reliable security is derived primarily from community protection. When communities value the lives and commitment of aid workers, they try to provide safe environments for those workers. Many humanitarian workers tell of being

In Hue, Vietnam, several Quaker humanitarians were sitting around their small house. Two international visitors were with them for a few days and were scheduled to return to Saigon later that week. A local friend stopped by. They drank tea and talked. As the friend left he quietly indicated that the two foreigners should change their plans and fly to Saigon the next morning.

The resident staff members knew their friend, and they arranged for the visitors to leave early. The next evening the Vietcong entered Hue and captured the city.

warned by a friend that it would be a good time to stay home or to take a brief holiday, only to find later that the warning had protected them from some outburst of violence.

Experience also indicates that transparency and openness can support staff security. In Guatemala in the 1980s, aid agency staff members were often under threat for supporting "subversive" activities of the "rebels" because they worked with poor rural people. Too often, locally hired employees would be "disappeared" by the army to intimidate people engaged in grassroots work.

When the assistant director of one agency was arrested in the marketplace one morning and never heard from again, the agency's expatriate field director's first tendency was to do what other agencies had done—namely, to assume an even lower profile to escape the notice of the authorities. Upon reflection, however, he decided to try a strikingly different strategy. He developed what he called "a light and sound show" of his agency's work, a slide show and speech that he presented "wherever someone would listen to me." He spoke to Kiwanis and Rotary clubs and to church groups. Pursuing a strategy of transparency, he took his presentation to the regional army headquarters and spoke with the commanders in charge of "antirebel" activities in the area. Over time, he found that even hardened fighters began to see the validity of his agency's work with peasants, and, more telling, no member of his staff was ever threatened again.

Finally, experience shows that in conflict areas total safety is simply impossible for either local people or for external aid agency staff. Providing aid in complex settings entails danger. When recruiting staff for emergency work, NGOs must acknowledge this reality and seek individuals who willingly take on the risk because of their commitment to service. There are many such individuals, and they, more than thrill seekers, are sensitive to the negative impacts of the implicit ethical messages cited here. The challenge for international aid agencies and their staffs is to maintain a careful balance between a willingness to take risks to provide aid and appropriate caution to avoid unnecessary risks that endanger themselves and others. The ability to maintain this balance grows from a deep belief in the value of life and of all lives equally.

6

Framework for Analyzing Aid's Impact on Conflict

Aid workers have learned many practical and useful lessons about how aid interacts with conflict. These lessons can be used to improve the planning, design, implementation, and monitoring of future aid programs in conflict areas. By using what has been learned through past experience, aid workers can ensure that future aid does not exacerbate or prolong conflict and that it does strengthen connectors and support local capacities for peace.

In this chapter we pull together the ideas and lessons presented in the preceding chapters into an Analytical Framework for Assessing Sources of Tension, Dividers, War Capacities, and Connectors and Capacities for Peace in conflict situations. This planning tool has emerged from interactions and discussions with aid agency staff in many areas.

Expectations for International Aid

To set the context for using the framework, we should first clarify expectations. What can aid do and what can aid not do in conflict situations?

The evidence clearly shows that aid saves lives, reduces human suffering, and supports the pursuit of greater economic and social security in conflict settings. This is what aid is intended to do, and overall the record is good. We expect aid to have these impacts.

But how realistic are we to expect that aid should also have positive impacts on conflict? What are its limitations?

Aid Neither Causes Nor Ends Wars

Even if aid workers applied the lessons of past experience and carried out perfect programs, wars would still happen. People and societies fight wars for their own reasons; outsiders cannot prevent wars. People and societies must achieve their own peace; outsiders cannot make or guarantee peace for anyone else. To arrogate too much power to aid, to operate as if aid can make war or bring peace would be to disrespect recipient societies' right and responsibility to choose.

As we remind ourselves of the limitations of international aid, two additional realities must be noted. First, whereas societies overall are responsible for their own warring or nonwarring decisions and actions, within societies many individuals and groups feel powerless in relation to those decisions and would, if they could, choose peace rather than war. Because this reality appears to be universally true, the dismissive comment sometimes made by international observers that "we should leave them alone to fight their own wars and not get involved" is inappropriate and fundamentally counter to humanitarian principles. Every society has people—often many people—who decry their country's wars and who value external aid because it enables them to express their opposition to destructive violence. Aid has a responsibility to respond to and join with these people.

The other reality that must be recognized even as we acknowledge aid's limitations is that even small amounts of aid have power. Although aid may be marginal when compared with the total resources devoted to wars, there is sufficient evidence showing its influence on the course of warfare that aid providers must take responsibility for its impacts. Aid's impact on conflict ranges from no effect at all to sizable and significant effects.

Some things happen in war on which aid has no effect. Some things happen that would happen regardless of whether aid existed, but because aid is provided in the context in which they occur it has an impact on them. In these circumstances aid workers must accept responsibility not for the fact that the events occur but for the ways in which their aid either worsens and prolongs destructive events or supports and strengthens positive ones.

Some events are caused by aid. When this happens, aid workers are challenged to ask if their aid has created new or increased tensions among people and whether it can help to restrengthen relationships or forge new connections among them.

In the complex conflict settings in which aid is provided, aid workers must be both realistic and humble enough to know what they cannot affect and what is not their responsibility, and they must be idealistic and bold enough to hold themselves accountable for the events they affect or cause. This is no small challenge.

Figure 6.1   Analytical Framework for Considering the Impact of Aid on Conflict

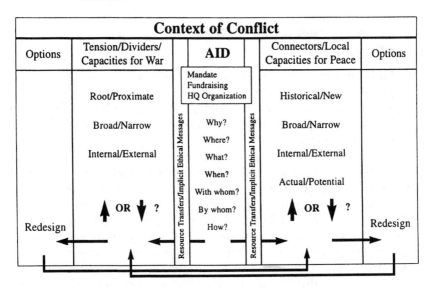

With this understanding of both the limitations of and possibilities for aid to influence conflict, we offer the analytical framework for planning aid programs.

Analytical Framework

International assistance can make conflict worse in two ways: It can feed intergroup tensions and weaken intergroup connections. When aid has either of these impacts, it inadvertently exacerbates conflict. Conversely, aid can help war to end by lessening intergroup tensions and strengthening intergroup connections.

Figure 6.1 depicts a framework for analyzing how aid interacts with conflict. The framework has three basic steps; it also prompts a dynamic feedback process for ongoing assessment of a situation and appropriate program redesign.

Step 1 involves identifying the dividers, tensions, and war capacities in the context of conflict and assessing their importance. Step 2 involves identifying, and assessing the importance of, the connectors and local capacities for peace in the same context. Step 3 involves identifying the pertinent characteristics of the aid agency and its program and assessing (and reassessing) their impacts on the dividers, tensions, and war capacities and the connectors and capacities for peace.

The Context of Conflict—Dividers, Tensions, and Capacities for War

Aid providers must first understand and assess what divides people, the tensions between them, and the capacities for war (who gains from it) in any area in which they are working. This is true whether the area is embroiled in open warfare or is prone only to low-level and occasional intergroup tensions.

Some dividers and tensions may be obvious. Warring parties often cite reasons for their wars. Histories of prejudice and exclusion, struggles for control of disputed resources, and differences in understanding how a just society should be organized are reasons people may go to war.

On the other hand, as we have seen, these issues may not underlie a conflict. Putative leaders may manipulate opinion and promote intergroup tensions, but the fighting may do very little to address systemic justice issues.

In assessing dividers and tensions, aid workers should differentiate between those that arise from injustice or historical inequalities and those that have been manipulated or that result from conflict itself. That is, aid workers should distinguish between root and proximate causes of conflict.

Not all sources of tension or divisions in societies have the same potential for damage. Some are local or matter to small numbers of people. Others reach across societies and involve virtually everyone. Aid's impact on dividers and tensions will vary depending on how broadly or narrowly they are shared.

Some tensions that are widespread may actually connect people on all sides of a conflict. For example, the common experience of lawlessness can add to overall suspicion and thus divide people, or it may motivate people to reach across conflict lines to reconnect in common cause against the threat of uncontrolled thuggery.

Some dividers and tensions exist within society, whereas others may be prompted and promoted from outside. Regional issues and external powers contribute to a number of current conflicts. Surrounding countries sometimes arm combatants for their own purposes (e.g., Afghanistan); events within neighboring countries sometimes spill into and destabilize another country (e.g., the Horn of Africa). The location of the source of conflict must be considered when assessing the potential impact of aid on dividers and tensions.

Assessing the importance of dividers, tensions, and capacities for war.   In this step it is important that aid workers not only identify dividers, tensions, and capacities for war but that they also assess their importance. A critical question is, Who is divided? Between or among which groups do the tensions or divisions exist? Tensions are often found within societies that although important do not overlap with an identity that would be likely to erupt into open conflict.

Additionally, in assessing the importance of dividers and tensions, aid workers should consider how deeply people are committed to their conflict. How widely is a commitment shared? Who gains from the continuation of conflict, and how widely shared are the gains?

Some important categories for identifying and assessing dividers, tensions, and war capacities (depicted in Figure 6.1) are root or proximate cause, broad-based or narrow involvement of people, and internal to society or externally induced. Aid's actual and potential impacts on dividers and tensions will vary depending on the depth and breadth of the commitment to war within the society in which aid is provided.

The Context of Conflict—Connectors and Local Capacities for Peace

Step 2 of the framework involves identifying and assessing connectors and local capacities for peace (LCPs) in the context of conflict. Whereas dividers and tensions may be overt and obvious, few connectors or capacities for peace are as readily apparent to aid workers, and they also vary widely in different contexts. It is insufficient to identify categories of groupings that might be connectors, such as elders, women's groups, or schools. Although in some settings such groups may bring people together in spite of war, in many societies they promote hatred and reinforce divisions.

Assessing the importance of connectors and local capacities for peace.   To identify genuine connectors and local capacities for peace in any specific location requires attentiveness to the actual systems, actions, and interactions in that setting. Questions to be considered are, What are the lines of conflict in which connectors and capacities for peace are important? Where do people maintain overt contact and connections across fighting lines? Where do people stay connected in less obvious ways? How widespread or limited are both the overt and the less obvious interactions?

Some important categories for identifying and assessing the importance of connectors and capacities for peace include long-standing, historical or new, as a result of conflict; broad-based, inclusive or narrow, an opening wedge; internal or external; and actual, existing or potential (can aid provide incentives?). Aid's ability to affect connectors and peace capacities will vary depending on these realities.

The Aid Program—Planning, Implementing, and Monitoring

Step 3 of the framework involves analyzing the aid agency and its program. Figure 6.1 depicts the aid program in three different places to emphasize the dynamics of the contexts in which aid is given and of aid programming itself. An aid program should be constantly reviewed as the context changes and as staff understanding of the context grows. Such review should prompt continual appropriate programmatic modifications.

The center column depicts an aid agency's initial intervention. Here we list all aspects of an aid agency that affect and shape its field programs. The agency's mandate, funding structures and sources, and headquarters' organization are relatively fixed regardless of field programs undertaken. (Note, however, that if field experience indicates that this core structure is counterproductive, even these aspects of an agency's identity can be changed.)

In addition, in any field effort aid agencies make a series of programming decisions. These include whether to intervene and why (stated explicit goal), where to intervene, what to provide, when and for how long, with whom (beneficiaries), by whom (field staff), and how. Some of these decisions are made at headquarters, some are shared by headquarters and the field, and some are made almost entirely in the field.

Decisions about whether, why, and where to intervene are usually made before an agency enters the field. Although they may be based on a field assessment mission, these decisions are made mostly at headquarters. Decisions about what to provide and the timing and duration of a program are often also dictated by donor policies and headquarters' mandates and structures. They are often shaped and adjusted, however, in response to field learning once a program is under way. Decisions about who shall be the beneficiaries of aid and what kinds of staffing should carry out a program are closer to the field, although international staffing patterns will be decided at headquarters. Finally, decisions about how to carry out programs are made primarily in the field. Although headquarters' policies may determine the shape and style of programming in general terms, staff in the field make local, specific, daily, and ongoing decisions about how they do their work. Decisions at every level can affect the impacts of aid on conflict.

The location of the various decisions between headquarters and the field highlights who has the responsibility and power to affect aid's interactions with conflict. People who make decisions at headquarters are responsible for the way their choices play out in the field. If the decisions have negative impacts, those individuals should assume responsibility. Likewise, people at the field level bear the responsibility and have options for determining how their choices affect conflict. Although the chain of decisionmaking is connected, individuals at each level always have options and latitude to ensure that their part of the process does less harm and more good. The entire system may not be changeable, but a thoughtful individual can adapt his or her part of the program to have a more positive effect.

Step 3 in the framework involves identifying the characteristics of an aid program according to the categories outlined and relating them to the analysis of the context (dividers or connectors) to anticipate how each programmatic choice will affect the context. For example, programmers should ask, Will a decision about staffing reinforce any division or tension we have identified? Will it feed into war interests? Or will it lessen tension? Can it support capacities for peace and connectors?

If staffing choices are seen as reinforcing divisions and tensions, it is time to consider the range of staffing options (options columns). Programmers should ask, How else can we staff this program? What about the number of staff? What types of people might we hire (men, women, all parties to the conflict, only one side, and so on)? What are the possible ways of working (paid staff, reliance on volunteers, working through government agencies, and the like)? Given what we understand about the divisions and tensions in this situation, how will each option affect them?

If the answer to reinforcing connectors is "no," one goes to the options column and considers all of the alternatives for staffing that might also build on and support connectors and capacities for peace. Programmers should ask, What do we know about local capacities and connectors? Can we devise a staffing pattern that will do the job and at the same time reinforce or reward a capacity or a connector?

The dynamic feedback elements of the framework require that each programming decision be checked through the two sides (dividers/tensions and connectors/LCPs). If staffing is adjusted to be sure tensions are not being made worse, the adjustment should also be tested against the connectors side of the framework. Programmers should ask, Is this the best we can do in terms of staffing choices not to feed tensions and at the same time support connectors? If not, is there another option?

Figure 6.2   The Impact of Aid on Conflict: Categories of Dividers and Connectors

Context of Conflict					
Options	Tension/Dividers/ Capacities for War	AID		Connectors/Local Capacities for Peace	Options
Redesign	Systems & Institutions Attitudes & Actions [Different] Values & Interests [Different] Experiences Symbols & Occasions ▲ OR ▼ ?	Mandate Fundraising HQ Organization Why? Where? What? When? With whom? By whom? How?	Resource Transfers/Implicit Ethical Messages Resource Transfers/Implicit Ethical Messages	Systems & Institutions Attitudes & Actions [Shared] Values & Interests [Common] Experiences Symbols & Occasions ▲ OR ▼ ?	Redesign

Similarly, if an option is found that reinforces connectors, programmers should recheck to see whether there is any way it will inadvertently reinforce a tension. If so, what other options exist?

The process is less complicated than it sounds. Once an aid provider has internalized the idea of dividers/tensions and capacities/connectors, she or he will always view choices through these lenses. It will become second nature to think about the inadvertent side effects of programming decisions in the context of conflict. It will remain primary to ensure that the agency's mandate and programming purposes are achieved. Additionally, it will become natural to consider how to do so in ways that do not exacerbate intergroup tensions but that support and strengthen connections among people as they build a just and peaceful society.

In Chapter 3, we identified a range of types of dividers and connectors, including systems and institutions, attitudes and actions, values and interests, experiences, and symbols and occasions. Figure 6.2 incorporates these categories under the two sides of the framework to remind aid workers to be attentive to the broad range of factors that their aid affects. If one were to merge Figures 6.1 and 6.2, it would be possible to identify a range of dividers, tensions, and capacities for war (or connectors and LCPs) and, then, to assess the importance of each of these in the terms depicted in Figure 6.1 (historical or new, broad or narrow, external or internal, etc.).

What a Framework Tool Does and Does Not Do

A framework tool does three things. First, it identifies the *categories* of information that have been found to be the most important in affecting the way aid interacts with conflict. Second, it *organizes* that information. Third, it highlights *relationships* among the categories and allows one to anticipate likely outcomes of alternative programming decisions. This facilitates an assessment of whether the anticipated impact is the best one available and if not allows an examination of options and alternatives to improve the impact.

A framework does not prescribe actions. It does not interpret events and factors for aid workers. It does not tell them what to do.

This tool, as with all tools, depends on its users' skill for its effect. But as is also true of all tools, a skilled worker can do better work with a good tool than without it.

How Much One Needs to Know to Use the Framework

It is important to begin any program design with an awareness of the context of conflict, including dividers and tensions and connectors and capacities for peace. Aid workers, however, will never know all of these aspects in detail and will certainly not know them when a program begins. Fortunately, they do not need to know everything at first.

They *do* need to be aware that some tensions are deep-seated whereas others are superficial, that aid itself can create new sources of tension if care is not taken to identify divisions in the society, that in all situations people stay connected through a range of factors that offer opportunities for aid support. With these three simple ideas and the motivation to look for and understand dividers and connectors, aid workers can design more effective programs.

Oddly, experience shows that people with long-standing knowledge of an area of conflict may not be in the best position to identify these elements and assess their importance. People who know "too much" often become mired in the complexities of the situation (which are real) and therefore lack sufficient distance to see opportunities for change. They see the present situation as inevitable. They often believe solutions can come only from outside, from external political actors. They can miss opportunities for local grassroots actions that support—and sometimes lead—political action.

Dynamic, Not Static

Earlier we emphasized the dynamic, iterative process of using the framework. It is also important to realize that a context of conflict is in constant change. Today's dividers may be tomorrow's connectors (as, for example, the common experience of war). New connectors may appear; new tensions may also appear. War itself often produces local capacities for peace. Aid workers should keep the categories in mind and be alert to change. They should regularly fill in the framework because using it can help to identify and highlight changes in reality—and in understanding—over time, which are important for effective programming.

In Part 2 of this book the framework is applied to six representative case examples of aid programming in conflict settings. These and other cases first illuminated the ways aid and conflict interact. We include them here both to illustrate how these ways emerged from varying realities and to demonstrate how the analytical framework can help us to understand the dynamic interactions of aid and conflict.

PART TWO

Local Capacities for Peace

Introduction to Part 2

Part 1 often refers to aid workers' experiences in conflict settings. These experiences and aid workers' reflections on them constitute the basis of the learning in this book.

In Part 2 we include five of the fifteen original case studies conducted by the Local Capacities for Peace Project. The fifteen case studies were carried out in Afghanistan, Bosnia and Herzegovina, Burundi, Cambodia, Croatia, Georgia, Guatemala, India, Jerusalem (Israel and the West Bank), Lebanon, Mozambique, Pakistan, Somalia (two cases), and Tajikistan. They provided the basis on which we identified common themes across many conflict settings, common problems aid workers faced even in different circumstances, and some ideas for creative programming alternatives to avoid doing harm and to ensure support of people's nonwar lives.

We selected the five cases to illustrate how the stories of aid, carried out in different places, suggest useful ideas for other aid programs. It was difficult to decide which cases to include because each is rich in local detail and thus provides a special lens through which to understand the relationship of aid and conflict.

We chose cases that involve different parts of the world (Burundi, India, Lebanon, Somalia, and Tajikistan) and different types of agencies (the International Committee of the Red Cross, a small indigenous NGO, a large UN agency, a small Catholic European NGO, and a large nonsectarian U.S. NGO). Different stages and types of conflict are included as well. Burundi and India represent conflict-prone countries in which intergroup violence occurs regularly but that have not experienced open civil war. The Somalia case covers aid during that country's period of active war. The Tajikistan case involves an aid program undertaken in the postwar period to support reconstruction in an effort to encourage repatriation. Four cases (Burundi, India, Somalia, and Tajikistan) describe how an aid agency pursued its mandated purpose but did so in a way that consciously addressed the fact that it was functioning in a conflict situation. Only one example (India) discusses an agency that faced regular violent disruptions of its ongoing program and added new activities to address the violence directly.

Each story is small and local. Each discusses a particular aid program, often located in just one section of a country and covering only a brief period of time. None resolves any of the major issues it raises, but each illustrates dilemmas encountered regularly when aid is provided in conflict settings. And more important, each suggests programming approaches that in some settings may ensure that aid not only accomplishes its mandated goals but also supports the people's attempts to establish a peaceful society.

7

Food for Work: Rebuilding Homes in Tajikistan

A Project of Save the Children Federation in Khatlon Province, Tajikistan

In early 1994 Save the Children Federation/U.S. (SCF) placed a staff person in Dushanbe, Tajikistan, to explore program opportunities to help Tajikistan recover from the violent civil war and economic dislocations that had followed its independence from the former Soviet Union.[1] The SCF field director wanted to develop a program that addressed immediate postwar needs and supported the reestablishment of peaceful relations among the former combatants. By 1995 (when this case study was written) SCF had a large and active program under way in several districts of Khatlon Province, one of the areas hardest hit by the war.

Background of the Country and the Conflict

Tajikistan is one of five Central Asian republics that gained independence with the breakup of the Soviet Union. Bordered by Afghanistan, China, Kyrgyzstan, and Uzbekistan, it was the poorest of the republics. When the Soviet Union collapsed, Tajikistan experienced a struggle for leadership that resulted in a civil war that lasted from May to December 1992.[2]

Different interpretations are given for the causes of the war. Elements of ethnicity, clan loyalty, religion, politics, and regionalism all played a role in the definition of alliances. The power struggle occurred between two groups—the former Communist leadership and what was referred to as *the opposition*—composed of the Islamists (the Islamic Renaissance Movement), the democrats (the Democratic Party of

Tajikistan), the nationalists (the Rebirth Party [Rastokhaz]), and the Lali Badakhshan Movement (a group claiming to represent the autonomous region of Gorno-Badakhshan).[3]

As was the case with all Central Asian republics, Tajikistan's borders had been artificially created by Stalin. Thus about 40 percent of the 5 million people in Tajikistan were non-Tajik and Turk in origin. Tajiks were of Persian origin and spoke Farsi/Persian rather than Turkish.

Because different ethnic groups aligned themselves to some extent with different power blocs, some interpreted the war as primarily an interethnic conflict. This was particularly the case in Gorno-Badakhshan, which declared its independence from Tajikistan, claiming its population—mainly Pamir Ismailis (an offshoot of Shi'a)—was ethnically different from both Tajiks and the other ethnic groups, which were mainly Sunni Muslims.[4]

Some believed the war arose primarily from regional conflicts, especially between the north and the south. The north, once a part of Uzbekistan and heavily populated by Uzbeks, was economically better off and more secular than other areas of the country. Its development had been achieved in part at the expense of the south; under Soviet rule the region is reported to have received a hundred times more capital investment than the south. During the civil war, the north was allied with the small Kulyab region in Khatlon Province, which spearheaded most of the conflict in that area.[5]

Others interpreted the war as ideological, reflecting differences between Islam and communism. Some believed it represented a pro-democracy movement against the former Communists who downplayed ethnicity and regionalism, citing their resistance to Islamic fundamentalism as the rationale for their fighting.[6]

Whatever the fundamental cause(s), the proximate history of the war began in spring 1992 after the opposition had forced former Communist President Rakhmon Nabiev out of power and taken control in Dushanbe. The new opposition leadership introduced Persian (with Arabic script) as the national language and began to emphasize Islamic influence, although it maintained that it had no intention of creating an Islamic state. The former Communists and their allies resisted, and war raged. By November 1992 the new government had been defeated, and the former Communists regained power.[7] The opposition was banned, and many people identified with it were killed or were forced to flee across the border to Afghanistan or to other regions of Tajikistan. Between 20,000 and 40,000 people were killed and nearly 500,000 were displaced—of whom an estimated 60,000 became refugees in Afghanistan and 80,000 massed along the border, unable to get across the river into Afghanistan.[8]

The Economy

As noted earlier, Tajikistan was the poorest of the Soviet republics. Under Stalin and subsequent Soviet administrations, production in Central Asia was concentrated on cotton and related enterprises (such as cotton milling, cotton seed production, and garment making). This virtually single-sector specialization meant Tajikistan depended on the other Soviet republics for most needed goods. Such economic interdependence meant that when the Soviet Union broke up, few republics were able to produce the range of required goods and suddenly needed foreign exchange to buy items previously allocated through the central authorities.

Cotton production in Tajikistan had been declining throughout the 1980s, even before the breakup of the Soviet Union, and with independence this very poor republic faced new and increasing economic difficulties that were greatly exacerbated by the war. Factories, equipment, and other productive infrastructure such as irrigation canals and roads were destroyed in the fighting. In addition, many skilled technicians and managerial personnel who were either Russian or were from other Soviet republics left Tajikistan because of the political instability.

Khatlon Province

One of the bloodiest areas of interethnic violence was Khatlon Province, located in the southwest Tajikistan and bordering Afghanistan. In this area the two major tribal-ethnic groups, the Kulyabi and the Garmi, fought each other as representatives of their respective power blocs. The Kulyabi sided with the former Communists, and the Garmi sided with the more religiously conservative opposition. Many people were killed, over 17,000 homes were severely damaged or destroyed, and many families fled for safety to Afghanistan and other parts of Tajikistan.

Although some Kulyabi homes were destroyed or damaged, most of the focused destruction and looting occurred after the former Communists had essentially defeated the opposition and many Garmi had fled. The Garmi also suffered more casualties than the Kulyabi, and the overwhelming majority of refugees and internally displaced persons (IDPs) were Garmi.

Once its victory was secured, the government of Tajikistan enacted policies to encourage the return of refugees and IDPs. The government declared that the occupied homes of people who had left (often Garmi homes taken over by Kulyabi families) should be returned to their owners. Although no functional legal system was in place to enforce this ruling, in a number of villages local elders (women and men, often Kulyabi) formed their own committees to oversee the smooth return of occupied houses. They were generally successful in diffusing tensions and reinstating the returning families to their homes within a few days or weeks.

Before the war the Kulyabi and Garmi had lived in apparent harmony in Khatlon. They were all Tajiks and as such shared a common language, culture, and religion. Both groups had been forcibly resettled in the area during the 1930s and 1940s to provide labor for the cotton farms, and although the patterns of their movement meant most villages were monoethnic, they had been vertically integrated through the collective farms and other state enterprises. Thus Kulyabi and Garmi had worked side by side and shared schools, clinics, and all other social services provided by the Soviet system. In towns and cities, intermarriage was not uncommon.

Drawing on their long history of interdependence, some people in Khatlon took reconciliation initiatives during the period of repatriation and return.[9] For example, a woman in the district government of Wakhsh responded to the return of a group of Garmi families by inviting some neighbors and some of the returnees to her home. She "prepared food for three days" and set a table for her guests in her garden. The returnees (Garmi) sat along one side and the people who had not left (Kulyabi) along the other. Facing each other across her table, they ate together in what she hoped was a reconciling way. In another village in Jilikul District, when Garmi families returned the Kulyabi residents "went out to meet them with bread and salt," a traditional symbolic welcome.

On the other hand, especially in the early days of repatriation, returnees often encountered direct hostility and reprisals. Some returning Garmi men were killed, families were threatened and beaten, and Garmi women and girls were raped. After a first wave of repatriation during which such events occurred, Garmi families adopted a new strategy of return. Acts of violence against women and children were less common, so Garmi men remained in refugee camps and sent their wives and children back home to begin to reclaim their homes and lives. After some months of an active United Nations High Commissioner for Refugees (UNHCR) protection program (during which UNHCR vehicles and staff were highly visible throughout Khatlon and staff members aggressively followed up every report of violence), the numbers of beatings and killings were greatly reduced and confidence rose. At this point Garmi men again began to return.

Many people in the province believed, as one UNHCR Tajik staff member put it, that "the common people don't want war, but the policy people make it." Some—both men and women—felt women had a particular role to play in overcoming animosity and reestablishing tolerance. Some described things ordinary people could do to overcome hostilities, including "training their children not to hate"; "teaching my children and grandchildren not to seek reprisals, not to keep remembering, and not to 'play' war with 'them'"; "working together on common projects"; and "getting my husband who was a schoolteacher to meet with 'their' schoolteachers to talk about how teachers from both groups can teach better attitudes in school."

Most, however, placed responsibility for the war and for peacemaking somewhere else. For example, many people said "time is the best healer" or "it will never happen again because people don't want it—we have learned (or 'they' have learned) our ('their') lesson."

Many noted that it was the "government's job" to make peace, an attitude that seemed in part to be a legacy of life under the Soviet system. Because independence had brought civil war and generally worsening economic conditions, many citizens from all ethnic groups and regions did not believe freedom or democracy had been worth the cost. Under the Soviet system the central authority had managed things and maintained order. In general, people had no experience with self-governance and independent economic entrepreneurship. Some noted that it had been a crime to undertake independent political or economic action when Tajikistan had belonged to the Soviet Union. They feared change could occur and that this sanction would again apply.

The International Response

ICRC and UNHCR

The International Committee of the Red Cross (ICRC) and the United Nations High Commissioner for Refugees were the first international agencies to enter Tajikistan in response to the war, placing staff in Dushanbe in December 1992 even before the hostilities had ended. The ICRC arrived first to work toward establishing conditions for peace and to monitor human rights. UNHCR arrived a short time later and quickly became the lead agency for the United Nations and other international agencies in Tajikistan. The UNHCR Representative also served as the Representative for the UN Department of Humanitarian Affairs (DHA).

From the outset, UNHCR interpreted its mandate for protection of refugees in what the Representative called a "proactive" way. Rather than limit coverage to returning refugees, staff members actively monitored and dealt with problems encountered by internally displaced persons and in some cases local people. As soon as the war ended, UNHCR encouraged the repatriation of refugees and return of IDPs to their prewar villages rather than waiting to see whether the peace was secure. To promote returns the staff made reconstruction a priority, providing timbers and roofing sheets for all families whose homes had been damaged.

Although protection and reconstruction were UNHCR's two main activities, the Representative also took an active role in the development of central government policies. As the lead UN official in the country, he was invited to the weekly meetings of the government's Council of Ministers, and in this forum he was able to help shape policies of repatriation and reconciliation. For example, the Representative was aware that official radio and television broadcasts often juxtaposed calls for "peace and reconciliation" with stories about monuments to the "loyal sons who fought against the enemy." He helped the government understand that it could not expect reconciliation to succeed if it continued to broadcast messages that labeled some citizens as "enemies"; the broadcasts changed as a result.

The UNHCR Representative invited the vice president to travel with him to Khatlon Province in a UN vehicle to see some of the problems people there were encountering. Before that visit the central government had relied on the reports of representatives who often provided misleading and inaccurate information that then became the basis of inappropriate government policies. After the field visit the vice president actively corrected false impressions in the capital city and set up approaches to gain more accurate information from outlying areas. Thus international aid's influence on the Tajikistan government's postwar policies was unusually strong and, according to most observers, positive.

NGOs and Save the Children Federation/U.S.

The NGO community was slow to enter Tajikistan, largely because of the uncertain security situation. Save the Children Federation/U.S. (SCF) was among the first NGOs to arrive when it placed an expatriate staff person in Dushanbe in spring 1994. As noted earlier, this staff member was eager to integrate SCF's humanitarian assistance and development work with reconciliation and peace-promotion efforts.

By fall 1994 SCF was fully operational with over fifty staff members, forty-five of whom were located in the Khatlon Province in the areas hardest hit by the war. Other NGOs quickly followed, and a variety of reconstruction programs were developed that focused mostly on rebuilding damaged assets, resupplying and rebuilding the health system, and developing small-scale economic enterprises and income-generating activities.

The SCF Program

In the early stages of its program exploration, SCF identified food insecurity and housing reconstruction as its priorities.[10] To benefit a broad spectrum of people beyond those who had lost their homes, SCF set up brigades of local people paid through Food for Work (FFW) to work as teams to rebuild destroyed houses. Roofing materials were supplied by UNHCR. SCF specified that everyone who wished to work for food could join a brigade, hoping thereby to ensure that both women and men could gain employment and that brigades would bring the Garmi and the Kulyabi together in a joint, mutually beneficial activity. FFW was important because it provided basic foods to families that otherwise faced serious shortages. SCF intended to follow this direct assistance program with a program of small loans and business management training to help create alternative income sources and fill the gap left by the barely functioning state farms and enterprises.

SCF hired over forty local staff members and an expatriate field director, all of whom were stationed in Kurgan Tuibe in Khatlon. Two expatriate staff members would oversee the programs from Dushanbe.

Local staff members began by visiting all villages that had suffered housing damage and carrying out a preliminary survey to assess damage and to gather demographic data about the numbers of returnees, average family size, male and female heads of households, and similar information. After "mapping" a village they held a community meeting called by local elders at which they explained the Food for Work program and invited villagers to set up as many brigades as they wished. SCF staff explained that both women and men were encouraged to join brigades and that membership did not depend on clan, ethnicity, or whether one's property had been destroyed. Everyone who wanted to work for food was welcome to join the brigades, which averaged between ten and twelve people each. When formed, each brigade elected its own leader who served as the direct liaison with SCF and was responsible for the assignment of jobs, the proper functioning of the team, the quality of construction, and distribution of food according to criteria set by each brigade.

In the beginning the community meetings were often chaotic, with everyone talking at once and vying for what they assumed would be limited resources and opportunities. As the meetings went on, however, people began to understand that everyone could be employed and that they would have a voice in the functioning of the brigade they joined. Having explained the formation of the brigades and the purpose of the program, SCF staff promised to return after several days to begin working with brigade leaders.

At their second meeting in each village, SCF staff met with the brigade leaders to assess the numbers and locations of houses to be rebuilt (based on findings from the preliminary survey) and to divide the jobs among the brigades. When these decisions had been made, SCF signed a contract with each brigade that specified the houses to be rebuilt, the exact amount of time required for the rebuilding (based on a formula developed by SCF that standardized rebuilding time according to extent of damage), and the precise amount of food that would be paid for the completed work.

The food provided included wheat flour and cooking oil, commodities that traditionally were in great demand in Tajikistan and that because of the generalized breakdown of Tajikistan's economy were in extremely short supply. SCF set the equivalent "wage rate" just below other market wages so people who had access to other resources or employment would not be enticed to join a brigade. The food earned by one person working in the reconstruction program in summer–fall 1994 was sufficient to meet 80 percent of an average family's caloric requirements through winter 1994–1995.

By fall 1994 the SCF program had successfully rebuilt a large number of houses before the onset of winter, which encouraged more families to return to their home villages than would have done so without this assistance. The program also provided much-needed food to many families. By January 1995 SCF was designing and seeking funding for a proposed credit and income-generation program.

Analysis of SCF's Impact on the Conflict

As noted earlier, one of the original intents of the first SCF field director in Tajikistan had been to promote reconciliation through the agency's postwar reconstruction program. By fall 1994, however, SCF had found opportunities to link housing with peacemaking elusive. Furthermore, locally hired staff articulated a clear demarcation between their work, which they defined as helping communities reconstruct their homes, and peacemaking, which they felt was "someone else's" responsibility.

Some of the difficulties with peace promotion had been anticipated. In its project proposal SCF had addressed possible negative side effects of its work. The agency recognized that because most of the destruction had occurred in Garmi villages, the majority of project resources would be directed toward only one side of the conflict. Anticipating that this targeting could "cause jealousy and reprisals by neighboring ethnic groups,"[11] SCF proposed adding a credit component to the program that by expanding the target group could "aid the process of reconciliation." The proposal went on: "Certainly SCF programme staff will be using that intervention as much as possible to rebuild understanding between ethnic/regional groups and to allay hostile tensions." In addition, SCF planned to include both Garmis and Kulyabis in the brigades and thus to spread the benefits of Food for Work across both groups. Finally, the agency planned to form some brigades around community projects such as rebuilding schools or clinics, again involving both groups in a project from which both would benefit.

None of these plans, however, successfully allayed intergroup tensions. A proposal for funding the credit program was under review in January 1995. The monoethnicity of the majority of villages (75 percent monoethnic and 25 percent mixed) and the fact that most damage had occurred in Garmi villages—coupled with the establishment of brigades within rather than across villages—meant both housing and food resources were channeled much more to Garmis than to Kulyabis. And because UNHCR's mandate limited the use of its roofing materials to homes of returnees, those materials could not be used for school or clinic reconstruction.

Further, allowing everyone in reconstruction villages who wanted to work to receive payment equal to 80 percent of a family's caloric requirements meant Garmi families could have more than one brigade member and thus receive more food than they needed. Since Kulyabi families had limited access to brigade work and to food, they resented the fact that their former enemies had a surplus of these much-needed goods.

As a result, SCF staff received complaints and in some instances direct threats from Kulyabi communities for "favoring the other side" through the FFW program. For example, one Kulyabi man pointed his *kalashnikov* rifle at SCF staff members, saying he would kill them if they did not rebuild his house instead of rebuilding all the Garmi houses. The senior staff person, a Garmi, agreed to go to the man's village to assess the damage. He found that several homes had been damaged, and he encouraged the village to form brigades to rebuild them.

The SCF staff members tried to encourage reconciliation in several direct ways. They formed some mixed ethnic brigades to clear and rebuild irrigation ditches and roadways. They hired staff locally and attempted to hire both Garmis and Kulyabis on the assumption that working together on a joint enterprise would both bring them together and demonstrate to others that cooperation was possible. They also felt their active presence in the communities reinforced stability and thus helped to establish conditions for reconciliation.

Upon reflection, however, SCF was aware that these measures did not offset the way its aid reinforced intergroup competition and suspicion. Further, the agency did not build on any of the networks and linkages in Khatlon Province that already existed between the two groups. For example, some staff members wondered whether they could have relied on the self-appointed housing reconciliation committees that handled occupied housing problems to set priorities for what should be built first and to communicate to the entire community why those priorities made sense. They further recognized that many people in the area, including the Kulyabi, wanted a return to normalcy and, in fact, depended on the return of Garmi families to ensure sufficient labor to restart cotton production. Given a strong common incentive to rebuild and restart the cotton farms on which everyone had depended, it might have been possible to open discussions among worker groups that would have resulted in a focused rebuilding of Garmi houses but with everyone's agreement that these families' return served them all.

8

Children in Civil War: Programming Toward Peace in Lebanon

A Project of UNICEF in Lebanon

Fifteen years of fighting in Lebanon hit Beirut with a vengeance in 1989 and 1990. Intense artillery and rocket fire ravaged the city. More than 60 percent of Lebanon's schools were closed in March 1989 because of the fighting, and they remained so for many months. Children and their parents were forced to take refuge in underground shelters for days and weeks at a time.

With the exception of a four-month relocation to Amman, Jordan, in 1976, the United Nations Children's Fund (UNICEF) maintained an active presence in Lebanon throughout the war. Providing emergency relief, immunization campaigns, and an essential drugs program, UNICEF became an experienced, trusted, and well-known organization, able to react quickly and effectively in a crisis and to reach into all regions of Lebanon in spite of the country's fragmentation. In 1989, however, traditional educational assistance became impossible because of the fighting, and UNICEF staff members were increasingly frustrated by both the terrible conditions children faced and their own inability to help those children as they hid in the shelters. The programmatic challenge facing UNICEF was to find a way to fulfill its mandate to support children's education and health in the midst of an ongoing and intensifying war.

This case was written by Greg Hansen for the Local Capacities for Peace Project in 1995 under the title "SAWA/Education for Peace: United Lebanon's Children and Youth During War." It has been edited and revised for this publication by Mary B. Anderson.

The War in Lebanon

Fighting in an already unstable Lebanon began in earnest in April 1975 and persisted with varying intensity until late 1990. As the war progressed, the dynamics behind the fighting and the effects of protracted violence and lawlessness grew increasingly complex, cyclical, and generalized. Over time, dozens of armed militias established complete control over various communities and thereby effectively undermined the power of legitimate government and the Lebanese state.[1]

Each militia and its parent faction claimed to represent the interests of a particular group; the Palestinian, Maronite, Druze, Shi'ia, Sunni, and other communities were all under the supposed protection of various armed factions. Other groups claiming ideological orientations also emerged. Ba'athist, Nasserite, pan-Arabist, Communist, quasi-fascist, and socialist factions formed their own militias. In some instances, primarily in the early stages of the war, ethnic and confessional (religious) groups were targeted for destruction or were purged from neighborhoods and villages. But the fifteen years of violence had an increasingly generalized and random quality that may ultimately have contributed to an awareness of its futility and, eventually, to its rejection by large numbers of Lebanese. Hostilities between factions claiming to represent the same groups accounted for much of Lebanon's violence, effectively undermining support from the very communities whose interests they claimed to represent.

Many of the militias had an economic interest in continued instability. By 1980 Lebanon had become one of the primary sources and transit points for opium, refined heroin, and hashish. Thousands of Lebanese depended on the drug trade for their subsistence.[2] In 1983 the livelihoods of an estimated 10,000 inhabitants of the Bekaa Valley depended directly on the hashish trade.[3] Drug profits were used to finance weapons purchases and to pay the salaries of private armies.

The larger militias maintained television and radio stations to propagate their versions of events and to stir up chauvinistic sentiments. Some established social welfare organizations for their own constituencies; many imposed systems of taxation in their zones of influence. Battles were fought over control of port facilities and the import tariffs they could provide. Lebanon was divided and subdivided into fiefdoms, with an ever-changing myriad of roadblocks and checkpoints serving as borders. Early in the war, Beirut was bisected by the Green Line, an area of frequent confrontation that became a swath of utter destruction dividing East and West Beirut.

Outside involvement in the war took many forms. Since 1948 Lebanon had absorbed hundreds of thousands of Palestinian refugees and become a site of much Palestinian political activity. Syria played an active role in the militarization of the Palestine Liberation Organization (PLO) and in 1976 intervened militarily in Lebanon. Parts of Beirut were subjected to heavy bombardment in 1978 as Syrian forces clashed with Lebanese militias. Following their own agendas, Libya and Iran also sponsored factions in Lebanon, and large amounts of weapons were shipped from Iraq to favored militias.

The Israeli Defense Force (IDF) invaded south Lebanon in 1978, prompting the deployment of troops of the United Nations Interim Force in Lebanon (UNIFIL). Lebanese militias sympathetic to Israel established the South Lebanon Army, creating for Israel a self-declared security zone along its northern border. After clashing with Palestinian fighters and bombing Beirut in 1981, Israel invaded Lebanon again in 1982 to drive Palestinian fighters and Syrian forces from Lebanon. Beirut was held under siege by the IDF, which was also fighting Syrian forces in the air and on the ground outside the city.

In 1982 a multinational force (MNF) made up of British, French, U.S., and Italian troops was committed to Beirut to oversee the withdrawal of Palestinian fighters, but the MNF itself was targeted. After some engagement U.S. forces withdrew, and the other MNF nations followed suit. In 1986 Syrian troops attempted a short-lived occupation of West Beirut, which led to more shelling by rival factions.

By 1987 the war had exacted a toll of over 120,000 lives, with another 10,000 killed after being kidnapped and 150,000 injured. As interfactional fighting continued between the Amal and Hizbollah militias in the predominantly Muslim West Beirut, East Beirut was also hostage to intense fighting between and among rival Christian-led factions and Syrian forces. In 1989 particularly brutal fighting targeted residential areas of Beirut and its environs from early March until the end of May and again from June to September. During this period between 4,000 and 5,000 shells landed each night in and around East Beirut.

Meanwhile, political efforts to end the fighting also intensified throughout 1989 and 1990. These efforts finally culminated in the National Reconciliation Charter (commonly known as the Taif Accord), adopted by fifty-eight of the sixty-two Lebanese members of parliament as a starting point for reconciliation. The charter contained provisions for a Syrian withdrawal, for the disbanding of all militias, and for the resettlement of Lebanese who had been displaced during the war. A state of relative calm has persisted since 1991, except in south Lebanon where attacks and reprisals frequently occur between the Hizbollah militia and the IDF–South Lebanon Army.

A 1988 study conducted by Mona Maksoud, director of psychosocial research for the Children and War Project at Columbia University in New

York City, examined the extent and forms of impact of the war on Lebanese children. The study found that 90.3 percent of the sample of children had been exposed to shelling or combat; 68.4 percent had been displaced from their homes; 54.5 percent had experienced extreme poverty; 50.3 percent had witnessed violent acts such as the intimidation, injury, or death of someone close to them; 26.0 percent had lost someone close to them; and 21.3 percent had been separated from their families.[4]

UNICEF in Lebanon

UNICEF had been active in Lebanon since 1948 when it assisted Palestinian refugees from the first Arab-Israeli war. In 1950 Beirut became the site of a regional office. In addition to its programming for refugees, UNICEF embarked on longer-term activities throughout Lebanon, including the promotion of public health, preventive health care policies, vaccinations, and maternal and child health care. UNICEF also provided training for social workers and assisted the Lebanese government, through the Ministry of Labour and Social Affairs, in establishing a school of social work. UNICEF's education program helped to establish kindergartens and train primary schoolteachers.

With the onset of the war in April 1975, UNICEF's orientation shifted to emergency assistance, including distribution of blankets, mattresses, clothing, soap, medical supplies, seed and fertilizer, food, and cooking utensils. Oral rehydration salts, vaccines, and other essential drugs were also distributed throughout the country through a network of dispensaries. UNICEF estimated that between April 1975 and September 1976 it provided emergency assistance to over a million Lebanese, more than a quarter of the country's population.

Reconstruction work, in cooperation with the government ministries, commenced in early 1977 and was focused on the public schools, social centers, hospitals, dispensaries, and other health facilities. UNICEF was also the lead agency, in cooperation with the government, for the rehabilitation of water and sanitation works damaged by the war. A total of 1,100 schools, kindergartens, social centers, and other institutions had received assistance under this operation by the end of 1979.

Over the next eight years, UNICEF assumed an increasingly prominent role in both relief assistance and regular programming. Through these activities UNICEF built an unparalleled logistics capacity and countrywide reach. No other agency enjoyed UNICEF's access to all areas of the country, and only UNICEF could elicit cooperation from all factions in its work. Three activities in particular added to the agency's countrywide recognition, public credibility, and freedom to act; they also gave agency staff important experience in social mobilization.

Operation Water Jug

In June 1982, as Israeli forces approached Beirut, the UN Secretary-General ordered the evacuation of all UN agencies. UNICEF stayed on, with one international officer remaining with the Lebanese staff.

The IDF imposed a seventy-day siege on West Beirut, with shelling and aerial bombardment. A blockade was imposed on the area, and water and electricity were shut off. At the height of summer, the risk of typhoid and cholera was high as people resorted to unsafe sources of drinking water.

UNICEF responded with Operation Water Jug. A small fleet of tanker trucks marked with the UNICEF logo was mobilized. Temporary reservoirs were set up in West Beirut and were replenished regularly by the fleet. Generators and pumps were mounted on trucks and driven to hospitals and tall apartment buildings to fill tanks on the roofs. Water was also provided for fire fighting.

Countrywide Immunization

Many factions had established social welfare systems in an effort to gain legitimacy among civilian populations. In some cases these services extended to the operation of clinics and dispensaries formerly run by the Ministry of Health. Against this backdrop, in 1987 UNICEF made a successful appeal for a nationwide immunization campaign. In the midst of factional warfare, UNICEF secured agreement to halt the fighting long enough to carry out four "national days of immunization."

To support the campaign UNICEF enlisted the cooperation of over 300 Lebanese NGOs, many of which were aligned with confessional groups or factions. In addition, UNICEF launched an aggressive public awareness campaign through the media to urge parents to bring their children to designated sites for vaccination. In the mosques and churches Islamic mullahs and Maronite priests urged participation. Faction leaders eased UNICEF's passage through dangerous areas, roadblocks, and checkpoints. Factions provided transport, equipment, food, and fuel for immunization teams.

Essential Drugs Program

By 1989 Lebanon's Ministry of Health had been crippled by its inability to gain access to most of the country. Prior to the war, a district-based network of clinics and dispensaries had served the population's needs, but many of them had fallen under factional control or been destroyed. As a consequence, no system was in place to distribute essential drugs.

Capitalizing on its ability to deliver countrywide assistance, UNICEF embarked on a program to rejuvenate the network of dispensaries by ensuring a regular supply of forty-four essential drugs. The drugs were obtained through UNICEF's international supply system and were emblazoned with the UNICEF logo. An estimated 75,000 people a month benefited from this program. By working with a number of local NGOs, UNICEF helped to sustain a network of about 750 dispensaries and clinics.

UNICEF's Other War-Related Programming

At the height of the bombardment of Beirut, UNICEF launched two additional programs for children that directly addressed their educational needs and the trauma they were experiencing from the effects of the war.

SAWA

"There were bombardments every night; our nights were spent in the basement, our days were spent trying to do something," recalls the UNICEF representative in Beirut during the 1989–1990 intensification of the war. UNICEF was carrying on successful programs in vaccinations and essential drugs, but the staff was frustrated because it was dealing only with adults and wanted to find a way to help children directly. The staff members asked themselves what they could do to reach the children in shelters. How could they do something for them now during the worst of the fighting? They knew parents often succumbed to the stresses of the war and were preoccupied with meeting basic survival needs. They knew the children were frightened and also bored because they had nothing to occupy their time except fear as they endured hours in the shelters. What kind of program could UNICEF initiate to address these circumstances?

During one bout of shelling, when the UNICEF staff members were sheltered in the basement of their office building, they decided to produce an "exercise book" for children in the shelters that could include stories, arts and crafts projects, arithmetic practice, and so on. Within a few days, they had published a mimeographed newsletter in Arabic for children. This edition—a few pages, stapled together—was "openly pirated" from French children's magazines, according to the Representative. (Later, when he wrote to the magazines to explain how their material had been used, they replied "God bless you!")

The next problem was how to deliver the newsletter to the children. As noted, UNICEF maintained regular contact with a network of clinics and dispensaries to distribute essential drugs. UNICEF issued public service announcements on radio stations telling children to have their parents go to the dispensary on safe days because "UNICEF has something fun for you and your friends there." The newsletters were loaded onto the trucks that carried the drugs and were dropped off at each clinic and dispensary as the drivers made their deliveries.

Three newsletters were produced and distributed over the following weeks, and the response was overwhelming. The newsletters disappeared from the dispensaries as quickly as they were delivered. UNICEF decided to formalize the program.

A project officer with experience in communications, education, and social mobilization was designated the head of a team to produce a magazine for Lebanon's children. She solicited donations for layout, typesetting, and illustration services from a large Beirut printing and graphics firm. She also recruited volunteers to write and draw for the magazine. Within seven days the first formal issue of *SAWA* (meaning "together" in Arabic) was ready to go to the printer.

The team head noted: "What we wanted to do was bring [children] together. . . . We wanted to build a nation on the recognition of common, universal values." Every issue was designed to take children beyond the context of war and the confines of the shelters. Issues were devoted to relaxation, space, nature and the outdoors, the world of work, the family, and the school. Later, they focused on other aspects of UNICEF's mandate—safe water, immunization, and UNICEF's summer Peace Camps (discussed in the next section).

SAWA had a number of regular features. A section called "Know Your Country" took readers on imaginary tours to Baalbek and the Cedars or across the Green Line in Beirut. The purpose was to remind children that they shared one country and to instill a sense of Lebanese identity. A similar feature, "From Our Culture," related Lebanese proverbs and folk tales or introduced an important historical figure from Lebanon's past, again to emphasize a common heritage. "Living *SAWA*" promoted a message of peace; the section included stories and parables illustrating children's rights, solidarity, unity, and nonviolence. "Right or Wrong?" gave the reader an opportunity to choose appropriate behavior in different situations. Creativity was encouraged through "Arts and Crafts" in which, for example, a child would be shown how to make a dozen different toys from something simple and available, such as an empty plastic water bottle.

Sharing was encouraged. Readers were asked to use *SAWA* with their brothers, sisters, friends, and parents, thereby expanding the magazine's reach and unifying influence.

With each issue *SAWA*'s content was determined increasingly by the children themselves. Following the distribution of the first issue, UNICEF received 1,500 letters from children thanking the agency and enclosing stories, drawings, poems, and jokes. From the second issue onward, *SAWA* contained two blank pages that could be used as a return letter. Here the child was invited to respond by writing a story, making a drawing, or whatever. Printed instructions on the pages told the child to take the letter back to the place where she or he received *SAWA,* and from there it would be forwarded (on the drug delivery trucks) back to UNICEF. UNICEF was soon receiving an average of 2,500 replies to each issue; selected responses were published in a new "Return Mail" section.

The contributions became an integral part of *SAWA,* and from this source of feedback *SAWA* began to take on a more overt peace orientation. Through *SAWA* children began spontaneously to express their yearning for a better life. Poems, pictures, stories, and prayers from the children talked about peace and possibilities rather than war and violence. One little girl suggested a "Pledge for Peace"; the pledge appeared in *SAWA*, and kids signed on enthusiastically.

In 1990 UNICEF undertook a survey to assess *SAWA*'s coverage. The survey revealed some problems with distribution, which the agency remedied by using the dispensaries as drop-off points for bundles of 50 to 150 copies. UNICEF field officers mobilized NGO partners and local scout troops, women's organizations, and sports clubs to distribute *SAWA.* Children's groups, crèches, playgrounds, churches, mosques, shelters, and other public areas were canvassed. Ten thousand copies were sent to the Palestinian camps. Children's responses had to be picked up and returned to dispensaries where they could be transported back to Beirut.

UNICEF field staff eagerly embraced the promotion of *SAWA* since it enhanced their relationships with the NGOs. Thus *SAWA* became an instrument of social mobilization.

SAWA was produced regularly until the end of the war in late 1990. Five issues were published in 1989, six in 1990, and a few in subsequent years.

Summer Peace Camps

SAWA provided a means of expression through which children could have vicarious contact with one another in spite of the physical and psychological separation imposed by the war. UNICEF's representative recalled that "sometimes kids were living across the street from one another but had never met." He and other staff asked what UNICEF could do to help prevent children from doing the same things their parents had done that had led to fifteen years of war. Roadblocks and checkpoints were only the physical manifestations of more profound barriers between people. UNICEF's program officer for education felt the answer lay in bringing children together to practice new attitudes and behaviors.

Remembering that before the war a group of NGOs and civic associations had supported a summer camp movement, the education officer notified fifty established NGOs (most with a confessional affiliation but one that predated the war) that UNICEF would support a renewed summer camp program for children from all confessions and regions of the country. UNICEF offered to provide funding, logistics, and training for camp animators if the NGOs provided the participants. UNICEF also guaranteed children's safe passage to the camps.

UNICEF asked the NGOs to agree to three objectives:

1. The camps would bring together youths of different regions, religions, and social status.
2. The camps would give youths and children a chance to get to know one another and to learn about their country through discovery and sharing.
3. Youths and children would live together positively, sharing human, social, and relational values through creative and recreational activities.

In stating these objectives, UNICEF was explicit about its peacebuilding agenda from the outset. By the end of May 1989, the NGO response had been overwhelmingly positive. Early July was targeted for the first camp to be held in the Bekaa Valley. A training session was designed for camp monitors ages sixteen to twenty-five. By the end of May a weeklong session had been designed, and the training was under way. The first two-week camp was held as scheduled, with 150 children in attendance from all over Lebanon.

The logistics and security arrangements were formidable. Project staff members were initially surprised that Christian parents were willing to send their children into Muslim areas for the camps. But the UNICEF name reassured parents, and in the interest of transparency a radio and television campaign announced the event to all of Lebanon. When parents showed hesitation, UNICEF staff responded by asking them to give their children a chance to try a different approach.

The UNICEF Representative never accepted negotiation as a means of securing passage for the children between militia strongholds. Instead of asking permission, he informed each faction leader of

UNICEF's plans to move busloads of children under the agency's flag. There were no problems.

As 1989 progressed, UNICEF built on the enthusiasm generated by its initial effort and in response to demands from children and parents, who welcomed the opportunity to get their kids away from the fighting, scheduled more Peace Camps. NGOs also organized day camps, with UNICEF managing the curriculum, the media, and other areas.

UNICEF staff observed that the younger children in the camps usually took a couple of days to be comfortable with "the other." For many, this was the first time they had met a Christian, a Muslim, or a Druze. Suddenly they were living, playing, working, and eating together in an unthreatening atmosphere.

The experience was carefully planned to provide an atmosphere of tenderness and caring, forgiveness and solidarity. A typical day involved working together on a common task such as cleaning their "homes" or planting trees. Awareness of and respect for the environment were promoted as a means of opening children's eyes to their surroundings. Games designed to encourage cooperation, sharing, and knowledge of "the other" were initiated by encouraging and supportive animators who made a point of nurturing contact between children from different backgrounds. Time was set aside for arts and crafts, singing, skits and dances, trips to historic sites, and hikes in the woods. Children were given T-shirts and caps with the Education for Peace logo and the caption "Together We Build Peace."

Project staff members were not surprised that children came together relatively easily, but they were surprised by the animators. The UNICEF Representative observed: "Many of the monitors had borne the brunt of the war. Many had served as militiamen. But they were so happy and excited. They had discovered something." During their training the change that came over those who had fought in the war was remarkable: "The more they had been extremist during the war, the more involved they became in the program. They were the most energetic young people in Lebanon."

Neither UNICEF nor the NGO participants made special efforts to involve former fighters in the project, but the program officer believed the project had special appeal for those young people: "Fighting was becoming . . . useless. . . . Like all other young people, they were keen to be useful. If we at UNICEF did something . . . for them, it was this: We gave them a chance to be useful. You have to look at why these young people fought. They weren't bad guys; they just thought they were doing something for their country."

The animators proved to be the backbone of the project and were seen by UNICEF as the major agents of change for peace. These young people came from all over Lebanon to learn to interact positively with children and to be constructive role models. Through UNICEF's training program they were given the tools and ideas needed for practical action in their communities.

In 1989, even as the war raged throughout most of Lebanon, 29,000 Lebanese children attended 34 summer Peace Camps and 79 day camps. One September celebration brought together 700 animators and 9,000 youngsters for a daylong Peace Festival in the western Bekaa. In 1990 around 30,000 youngsters attended 155 day camps and 60 summer camps, as well as a number of camps organized by NGOs with support from the project. By September 1991 UNICEF had reached 100,000 children and mobilized 240 NGOs as partners in the program, which included the entire spectrum of confessional, ethnic, and regional groups in Lebanon.

Analysis of UNICEF's Impact on the Conflict

SAWA and the Peace Camps were inseparable from the context that produced them.[5] With UNICEF as the capable facilitator, each program was able to give expression to a powerful but previously dormant will for peace among Lebanon's youth in the midst of the violence of war.

As is the case with such bottom-up approaches, it is difficult to assess whether and how the projects affected the conflict. The experiences nurtured by *SAWA* and the Peace Camps were largely individual and subjective, as they were designed to be—which does not necessarily render them unimportant in terms of their potential contribution to the achievement of peace. In fact, the numbers of people involved in all of UNICEF's programs attest to the agency's impact on many people's lives and to the consequent likelihood of its significant impact in coalescing, if not shaping, broad opinion and action.

The UNICEF experience in Lebanon points to several important and potentially useful ideas for relief and development programming in conflict settings.

Within Its Mandate, Drawing on Its Experience

UNICEF was able to develop a creative and appropriate programmatic expression of its mandate in the midst of the violence of war. UNICEF built on its experience and resultant countrywide credibility, access, and ability to elicit cooperation from a broad range of factions to pursue its own (rather than their) agenda. Rather than taking a political antiwar stance, the programs were undertaken and justified as expressions of UNICEF's mandated concern for the health and education of children.

> Tolerance for peacebuilding activities involving the young may emerge out of a genuine wish to give them a chance to do things differently, or because children constitute a "zone of peace" in their own right, or simply because the activities of young people are not taken altogether seriously by adults. Whatever the reason, such activities may open doors for expanded peacebuilding activities or have "spin-off" effects, and thus may be seen as an effective means of initiating a larger peacebuilding process (e.g., child to child, child to youth, youth to youth, youth to adult, adult to adult).[6]

Providing Space and Expression for Nonwar Attitudes and Actions

UNICEF provided space for many people to act and think in nonwar ways. The agency also provided fora for people to express nonwar attitudes and behaviors. It did this even as war shaped all other aspects of life in Lebanon—at the height of the violence—rather than when it was relatively easy to do.

Fighters and warlords used the airwaves to propagandize for their causes. UNICEF regularly used Lebanon's radio and television networks to maintain transparency in its programming and to encourage people to become involved in the alternatives it offered. These public service announcements were seen as nonpolitical and thus were allowed by the fighters.

Linkages can be forged between providing assistance in response to commonly experienced needs, on the one hand, and giving beneficiaries an opportunity to express their desire for alternatives to violence on the other. This was demonstrated by both the linkage between *SAWA*'s stated goal of providing an educational tool for children who were unable to attend school and the theme of togetherness that dominated the magazine and the linkage between the Peace Camps' stated goal of giving young people a summer recreational experience and the promotion of inclusiveness and the inculcation of constructive values.[7]

UNICEF also provided space for its staff members to work across factional lines. They judged this to be a privilege of working for an agency such as UNICEF because it gave them access to all parts of the country. This situation allowed them to identify themselves first as "Lebanese," even when all other pressures were forcing people to identify themselves according to factional subgroups.

Many agencies that worked in Lebanon during the war provided evenhanded aid among factions, trying to maintain a balance in what they did for different sides. UNICEF provided assistance on the basis of a group's capacity to deliver—to cooperate in pursuing a common goal: "Beginning with personal contacts and working outward, project staff engendered a spirit of collegiality and cooperation with a diverse collection of partners."[8] Staff members continually demonstrated that people who disagree on some things can nonetheless collaborate on important issues of common concern.

The "Right" Program at the "Right" Time

A certain readiness must be present within a population for social mobilization efforts to strike a chord.[9] UNICEF staff members recalled that conditions were so bad in Beirut in 1989 that parents would drop their chauvinistic sentiments when given the chance to get their children out of the city.

According to one UNICEF staff member, the pivotal moment for many Lebanese in terms of disengagement from the conflict was the closure of schools in 1989. The value placed on education in Lebanese culture is so high that when the fighting indefinitely interrupted children's schooling it was the final straw for many. Others thought UNICEF's project struck a chord because "enough is enough"—after fifteen years of war the younger generation was ripe for change.

9

Norms of Humanitarian Conduct: Disseminating International Humanitarian Law in Burundi

A Project of the International Committee of the Red Cross in Burundi

Burundi is small, densely populated, and landlocked. Yet it is an extremely fertile land in which 95 percent of the almost 6 million inhabitants live in rural areas and are involved in agricultural production. Hutus make up about 85 percent of the population and Tutsis about 14 percent.

Confronted with widespread violence in Burundi in the wake of the attempted coup d'état in October 1993, representatives of international relief agencies were faced with the question, Can we do anything to introduce a measure of restraint into the minds of fighters or to support the determination of people who do not want to participate in the vicious cycle of killings? The question was particularly challenging for the International Committee of the Red Cross (ICRC) since one of its mandated tasks is to promote and disseminate International Humanitarian Law (IHL) and fundamental humanitarian principles. The goal of dissemination is to create respect for IHL and fundamental humanitarian principles in situations of armed conflict and internal violence.

This case was originally written by Lena Sallin in June 1995 with funding from the Swedish Red Cross. It has been revised and edited for publication in this volume by Mary B. Anderson.

The Context of the Conflict in Burundi

In the fifteenth century cattle-owning Tutsis invaded Hutu-dominated Burundi, subsequently establishing a feudal relationship by making their cattle available to the Hutus in exchange for work and taxes.[1] The colonial rule of Germany (1885–1916) and Belgium (1916–1962) reinforced Tutsi dominance because Tutsis were relied on for daily administration.

After independence in 1962 Burundi remained a monarchy until 1966, when a military coup turned the country into a republic. Three military regimes, all Tutsi, followed. Traditional Burundi society is conservative and hierarchical but, paradoxically, is socially coherent in the sense that Hutus and Tutsis speak the same language—Kirundi—have the same lifestyle and religion (most are Catholics), intermarry, and maintain strong social relationships. Because of their dominance, however, Tutsis have always had greater access to education, economic resources, and employment.

During the period of successive military coups, political tension between Hutus and Tutsis emerged. Numerous, although isolated, outbreaks of interethnic violence took place. In spite of this, Burundi remained relatively stable politically until 1993. Since 1993 a series of crises has eroded state authority and led to political instability.

The deterioration that led to this situation is generally considered to have resulted from the democratization process initiated by President Pierre Buyoya in the 1980s. Buyoya seized power from his predecessor in a bloodless coup in September 1987. He initiated a series of democratic reforms including the enactment of a Charter of Unity (1991), the drawing up of a new constitution (1992), and the creation of a cabinet structure in which Hutus would hold half of the seats (nominated in 1992). These reforms culminated in the first free presidential elections, held on 1 June 1993 when Melchior Ndadaye, leader of the predominantly Hutu Front for Democracy in Burundi (FRODEBU), became Burundi's first democratically elected president. In the first free parliamentary elections that followed, FRODEBU won a landslide victory with 78 percent of the votes.

Following the FRODEBU victory the political tension between Hutus and Tutsis gradually deepened. Tutsis lacked formal power but controlled most of the state apparatus, including the police and the judicial system; they also completely controlled the army. For the first time Hutus, the majority population, held formal power but lacked control over the important institutions.

Only three and a half months after these reforms, the democratization process was violently halted by an attempted coup d'état by a minority of military extremists. President Ndadaye and a number of high-ranking government officials were assassinated. Following the assassinations a wave of interethnic violence resulted in the deaths of between 50,000 and 100,000 people and in the internal displacement of almost 300,000 people. More than 600,000 others fled to Tanzania, Rwanda, or Zaire.

Cyprien Ntaryamira, who succeeded Ndadaye, was killed, along with Rwanda's president Habyarimana, when their plane was shot down over Kigali in April 1994. This event did not, as was feared, bring a recurrence of ethnic violence in Burundi; further, the violence between Hutus and Tutsis that followed in Rwanda caused no mirror response in Burundi. One factor in maintaining peace was a government campaign to calm people's feelings by touring the country and calling for restraint.

The increasing intergroup tensions, the power imbalance, and the series of crises provided fertile soil for influential and power-hungry politicians. Both sides set Hutus and Tutsis against each other, inciting fear of "the other" by preaching the need to protect one's own and painting horrific pictures of what might happen to those who did not protect themselves. Throughout 1994 and 1995 extremist politicians on both sides became increasingly hard-line, and new armed groups emerged that escalated the forms and extent of violence.

In spring 1995 bands of Tutsi youngsters, armed by extremist politicians, took the law into their own hands and ruled the streets of Bujumbura with no apparent motive other than to demonstrate their power to do so. At the same time, the number of armed Hutu groups in the countryside increased.

In March 1995 the tension in the country again erupted into uncontrollable massacres, first in Bujumbura and later in the northern provinces. Two of Bujumbura's remaining mixed quarters were "cleansed" of "the other" ethnic group. Hundreds of people were killed, and tens of thousands fled the capital for Zaire and the northern provinces for Tanzania.

In April the government undertook a one-month reconciliation campaign. On a tour of the country led by President Sylvestre Ntibantunganya, the ministers answered provocative questions from citizens in sessions closely followed by the press, radio, and television. The quiet did not last long, however, and violent clashes again flared up in June and July.

These events shaped the context in which international aid agencies worked, and they prompted—and affected—a decision by the International Committee of the Red Cross to try a new direction in its programming.

The International Committee of the Red Cross

The International Committee of the Red Cross (ICRC) is an independent humanitarian organization based in Geneva that was founded in 1863. It is the founding body of the Red Cross Movement, which also includes the International Federation of the Red Cross and Red Crescent Societies, as well as more than 160 Red Cross and Red Crescent National Societies throughout the world.

The ICRC's mandate, granted by the Geneva Conventions, is to provide protection and relief to victims of international and noninternational armed conflict[2] or internal disturbances and tension,[3] continually promoting and disseminating International Humanitarian Law and fundamental humanitarian principles.[4] The traditional target groups for dissemination are governments, officers and instructors in the armed forces, academic and scholastic communities, National Red Cross and Red Crescent Societies, and national media—with the common denominator these groups' capacity to spread the message.

The 1949 Geneva Conventions apply to wars between states and are not formally applicable to the situations of internal conflict that characterize most recent conflicts.[5] In these situations human rights conventions are often derogated through a declaration of a state of emergency, leaving combatants and civilians without legal protection except the hard core of human rights—the essence of which has been integrated in Article 3—common to the four Geneva Conventions. The ICRC and other experts on IHL have long considered ways to formulate rules that would be acceptable to all parties and that could be applied in all types of conflict situations, including those in which the line between combatants and civilians is blurred. Apart from highlighting the need for such rules, the complex and multifaceted conflicts that followed the end of the Cold War prompted the ICRC to develop a wider concept and alternative methods of dissemination.

Traditional dissemination had been based on a judicial framework of humanitarian norms, an approach that did not attract the majority of civilians. To improve the impact of its humanitarian message and reach a larger audience, the ICRC has recently developed a new approach to dissemination that considers the culture and traditions of the country in question when formulating its message. This approach uses local articulations of the local values of people in conflict to highlight and explain the fundamental humanitarian values contained in IHL.

The ICRC in Burundi

Until 1990 the ICRC maintained a sporadic presence in the Great Lakes region (Rwanda, Burundi, Zaire, and the northwestern corner of Tanzania)—visiting security detainees, promoting IHL, and supporting National Red Cross Societies. When war broke out in Rwanda in 1990, an ICRC delegation was established in Kigali, and a small office was set up in Bujumbura. In October 1993 the ICRC had one delegate in Burundi who was mainly involved in tracing activities. After the events of October 1993, the ICRC increased its staff of expatriates in Burundi to six in November and to sixteen in December.

Initial activities focused on providing emergency medical care and evacuating the wounded. The ICRC wanted delegates in as many locations as possible throughout Burundi to reduce tension between the parties and to increase protection of noncombatants. When the emergency phase ended, the ICRC distributed nonfood items to internally displaced people, organized tracing activities, arranged for the exchange of Red Cross messages, and visited detainees.

Challenges

Most Red Cross delegates (as well as those from other organizations and, indeed, the Burundians themselves) felt disillusioned in the wake of the attempted coup d'état and the subsequent killings of between 50,000 and 100,000 Burundians.[6] The dissemination of fundamental humanitarian principles in this context seemed absurd. "Who would be able to promote International Humanitarian Law and the Red Cross principles in a context where the church is completely disoriented after decades of Christian sermons?" one delegate asked.

In November 1993 the ICRC dissemination delegate nonetheless held a dissemination session at a college in which some students had been involved in molesting and beating civilians. Many of the students had lost family members during the violence. They completely rejected the ICRC message about basic human rights and mutual respect.

"The young people not only refused to listen to our message but challenged us vehemently. 'You don't understand,' they said. 'You cannot understand because you have never experienced such a disaster in your own life,'" recalled another ICRC delegate. Traditional dissemination methods would not work in this environment.

One ICRC delegate was particularly concerned with finding an appropriate dissemination strategy. While traveling around Burundi, she asked many people what they needed and was encouraged when they asked for leadership rather than food. In December 1993 ICRC/ Geneva sent a delegate to Burundi to help staff there consider options for dissemination. In a meeting the ICRC convened, to which twenty Burundi intellectuals were invited, including sociologists and psychiatrists, the delegate suggested they formulate a Code of Conduct adapted to conditions in Burundi.

The members of the group immediately rejected the proposal. They felt other texts aimed at reconciliation and cooperation had failed to calm people and that another attempt, particularly if initiated by expatriates, would probably make no positive difference. Three people at the meeting disagreed. One was the ICRC delegate who had heard people ask for leadership; the other two were Burundians—one a freelance media consultant and the other a human rights activist.

The ICRC delegate began to study Burundian traditions and folklore. She also met with Burundians from all social and political groups.

> I did not think that we should content ourselves with merely a text. I thought it necessary to go further, but a text targeted toward all civilians would have to be the beginning. I wanted to find something that would appeal to people's understanding. I discussed [issues] with everybody I met, tested ideas, and talked for hours with representatives of different interest groups, different ethnic groups, different political parties, and different lines of thinking.

Dissemination

Finally, it was agreed that a dissemination program should be tried that would have the following features.

- The first goal should be to develop a text, a Code of Conduct, that would be built on in different ways.
- The text should emanate from a mixed group of twenty to twenty-five civilians driven by a humanitarian (rather than a political) ideal. The members should not be involved in politics.
- Everyone should clearly understand and accept that the purpose of the text is purely humanitarian.
- It must be equally clear that the purpose of the program is not to stop conflict or forbid people to participate; there must be no appearance of sociopolitical interference.
- No references will be made to politically tainted concepts or to any particular type or style of government.
- The text must be derived from the humanitarian traditions of Burundi.

- The text should be addressed to all Burundians and be worded so it can be understood by all.
- The text should be pragmatic rather than universal; that is, it should appeal to behavior in Burundi rather than to theories or hypotheses.
- Specific violations of humanitarian norms in Burundi should be named and related to directly.

When the criteria were set and the support of government officials and the army had been secured, twenty-five individuals were invited to participate in a working group to develop the Code of Conduct. Criteria for participants follow.

- They must not be in the government or the army or occupy higher posts in the hierarchy of the context in which they are working.
- They should have shown publicly an inclination toward or interest in humanitarian issues.
- They must not be a media personality or well-known in any other way.
- They must not be part of any defined group suspected by either side to have some responsibility for the ongoing violence.

The working group also had to be balanced ethnically and in affiliation to the two principal political parties.

The group first met in March 1994; between March and July, when it gave the first public presentation of its work, the group held thirty-four meetings. Throughout the process the ICRC kept government, army, religious, and political officers informed, thereby hoping (successfully) to maintain interest and minimize the risk of rejection once the work was completed.

The group produced a Declaration, illustrated by sixteen Burundian proverbs selected to create a sense of recognition and to facilitate understanding of the proposed rules. The group started with the fact that African tradition had guaranteed protection for victims of conflict long before the existence of IHL. In Burundi war was considered noble and was carried out in accordance with well-established rules and principles. Only members of the aristocracy could be warriors, and a young soldier was expected to possess courage, honor, discretion, prudence, and solidarity.

The Declaration set out "minimum rules of humanitarian behavior" under four categories:[7]

1. Let Us Respect and Protect Individuals and Their Dignity
2. Let Us Give Special Protection to Certain Categories of Victims
3. Let Us Respect Private and Public Property
4. Let Us Use Force only with Moderation

The rules were formulated to highlight the humanitarian principles that had most often been violated in the Burundian context.

For example, the first section contains rules such as:

- Let us treat every person with humanity and respect his or her dignity in all circumstances.
- Let us not be vengeful; let justice take its course. A spiral of violence would gradually destroy the whole family, clan, and community.
- Torture and cruel, humiliating, or inhumane treatment can in no circumstances be honorable; let us never use them against our fellow, even if he is our enemy.
- Let us never have recourse to brutal acts such as rape, mutilation before or after death, or killing by throwing people into latrines or burning them alive. Such manifestations of blind hatred leave indelible mental scars.

Thus this section reflected the spirit of Article 3 of the four Geneva Conventions and directly referred to atrocities that had been committed in Burundi.

The second section also drew on the spirit of Article 3. It declared that civilians, foreign nationals, refugees, women, children, the elderly, the disabled, the sick, prisoners, and medical personnel should be protected at all times. The text referred to these groups as defenseless, a direct reference to Burundi tradition in which it was considered cowardly to attack defenseless persons. Traditions held that women, children, and the elderly must never be killed in fighting and that killing women was paramount to an attack on life itself.

The third section related to the humanitarian principles of refraining from destroying people's means of livelihood and safeguarding places that had religious or cultural value. Protection of the religious and cultural heritage is spelled out in the Hague regulations. In Burundi tradition many sacred places were seen as objects of respect and were safeguarded in times of war.

The fourth section also drew on Article 3 and the ban on arms that cause unnecessary suffering contained in the Hague regulations. Burundi tradition strictly restricts the use of poisoned spearheads and ambush in certain contexts.

The conclusion of this section reads (in part): "Let us remember that each person is individually responsible for his acts, even those committed as part of a group or encouraged by someone else."

The importance of the proverbs was described by a member of the working group: "It was an excellent idea to use our traditional proverbs. They summarize in one or two lines what would otherwise have to be said on two pages of text . . . we have combined short rules in simple language with proverbs that sum up the issue. When we Burundians have a conversation, we often start or finish with a proverb, so this is a structure every Burundian citizen can relate to."

The Declaration was printed in both Kirundi and French. Radio spots that gave the text were produced and aired. A song that carried the message of the Declaration was recorded and also aired on Burundi radio. A twelve-minute video displaying dramatic pictures of the nationwide results of the outbreak of violence in October–November 1993, accompanied by the voice of a narrator reciting the rules of the Declaration, was produced.

A Public Forum

When all of this was done, the next step was to organize an event that would have a major impact at the national level and generate widespread interest in and national consensus for the program. The working group decided to organize a Video Forum. Many people from all social groups in Burundi were invited. The forum involved a week of presentations, during which each group had a two-hour session in which the Declaration was introduced, the video shown, and questions discussed. More than 600 of 1,000 invitees attended; thirteen two-hour sessions were convened. The sessions were attended by representatives of the local authorities in Bujumbura; diplomats; representatives of local and international NGOs, the clergy, and the political parties; teachers from primary and secondary schools; representatives of youth movements, the academic community, the National Assembly, business, and the armed forces; functionaries from the provinces; and "personalities," including government ministers.

Each session was introduced with the statement: "These norms for humanitarian behavior, worked out by Burundians and adapted to Burundi society, are a contribution to the reduction of the horrors created by the violence. They are not to obtain a general value until they are widely disseminated and taught. The program now belongs to all Burundians who accept it. It is for you to maintain it and to give it life." This was followed by presentations on the ICRC, International Humanitarian Law, and the origin, objectives, and contents of the Declaration.

As an introduction to the discussions, the unsentimental twelve-minute video of the aftermath of the 1993 violence was screened. The deliberate mix of pictures of destruction and sorrow with words of positive commitment pulled the participants into lively and heated discussions.

During the week of the Video Forum, the radio spot summarizing the Declaration and the song written to reflect the spirit of the Declaration were aired regularly on national radio. Moreover, national TV and radio summarized the events of the forum each day during the week.

Follow-Up and Outcomes

The Video Forum generated a positive response, and many people declared their intention to do something to help implement the rules. After the forum, however, very few Burundian associations actually did anything, and only one group, the Burundi Scout Movement, secured a promise for funding a Humanitarian Caravan that would tour every village in the three central provinces screening the video and distributing pamphlets. The organization that promised the funding left Burundi, however, and funds did not materialize. The scouts did work on an adaptation of the Declaration for young children.

Other agencies did not become actively involved because continuing violence and instability meant that agencies promoting reconciliation were often threatened. Nonetheless, the ICRC arranged with the education ministries and the university administration to integrate the Declaration into curricula. A brochure with a tale, testimonies, and an interview with an ICRC delegate plus proposals for pedagogical activities were produced for the upper primary school grades for introduction into all schools in 1995. The Ministry of Secondary Schools agreed to air the video to introduce the norms of the Declaration in civic education, and a teachers' discussion guide was prepared. At the university level, a document containing the IHL and customary law of the region was produced for the compulsory civics course.

Use of Theater

Prior to the Video Forum the working group had asked a theater group in Bujumbura that had members from both ethnic groups to produce a play reflecting the ideas of the Declaration. The group accepted, and the script writer set to work. The play was later developed into a sixty-five-minute film-video version. Theater had no place in traditional Burundian society, but since the violence it had become very popular, possibly because of Burundi's strong oral tradition.

The play revolved around a married couple in a village in the Burundian countryside. The husband and wife were from different ethnic groups, and when the villagers were incited by the "outside" to take up weapons against each other, the family and their friends were affected. The play covered all of the issues of the Declaration and was easier to understand than the printed version. Opening night in October 1994 drew a full house, an audience of 300. Six shows were staged during the following weeks, then the live performances stopped. The director of the play recalled:

We had planned more shows, but the reality stopped us. We started to receive veiled threats soon after the opening night. Extremists from both sides said that it was "stupid" of us to perform a play like this in the current circumstances. The fact that both Hutu and Tutsi actors are in the group made it difficult for us to perform in the same area. Not a single actor, however, regretted participating in the play. The fact that the actors agreed to play the role of someone from the other ethnic group, knowing full well that it would subject them to threats from within their respective ethnic groups, shows they were committed to the issue and ready to accept the anticipated criticism and possible danger.

The play turned out to be more successful than any of us had dared imagine. People recognized their everyday lives and were reminded of what had happened in their own families. Men and women alike reacted very strongly. Even the extremists on the fringes showed a lot of feeling. The audience was sometimes in tears.

I am convinced that the story has a great impact. Something is left in the heart of each spectator—remorse, perhaps, or determination. It will be much more difficult for someone who has watched this story to participate in the crimes. Next time he will think twice before he kills.

In the play, women from both ethnic groups played a major role in changing, or trying to change, the minds of the men and adolescents. The director explained:

The importance given to women in the play is deliberate and is part of the message. If women had more opportunity to speak their minds in our culture we would have a different society and would probably live in peace. Unfortunately, women are mainly expected to shut up in public.

But the role of women in Burundi is more complicated than that. They are responsible for bringing up and educating the children and are respected for that. They also advise their husbands but always at home, never in public. Men do not listen to women when other men are present. In the play, however, women are allowed to talk and to try to persuade and convince men.

From mid-December 1994 until the end of April 1995, a new ICRC dissemination delegate toured the Burundian countryside screening the twelve-minute video and the sixty-five-minute film-video version of the play in schools, churches, and assembly halls. He conducted over thirty screenings for more than 20,000 people in small villages across Burundi. The delegate reported:

> I believe the combination of the twelve-minute video and the play leaves a 100 percent imprint on people's minds. People are tired of violence. They want to live in peace. After having observed the reactions to the video and the play I am convinced that what we are doing supports moderate thinking and makes it more difficult for the extremists to incite the grassroots to kill one another.
>
> We show the film/video in remote places where there is no electricity, that is, no television. It is often the event of the year. The villagers talk about it for months afterward. They are hypnotized by the story. It makes a deep imprint on their mind. They learn the story and repeat it to others. If someone tries to encourage them to take up weapons and fight, I hope they will refuse. People identify with the characters and the story. It is reality to them, not a story.
>
> About a quarter of the screenings have been mixed. I couldn't tell the reactions of one ethnic group from the other. There are always comments like "moving," "instructive," "enlightening," and "informative" regardless of which group the audience belongs to. I am always asked to return for another session in the same or a nearby village.

The delegate conducted most of the field trips alone, taking along a generator, a jerrican of diesel, an amplifier, a film-video projector, a screen, videotapes, boxes of pamphlets, and blankets to cover the windows during the screening. Although the original plans emphasized the involvement of Burundians in implementation, the ICRC believed the situation was too dangerous and volatile to allow locals to tour the countryside. In part because of the danger to local people, the ICRC doubled the expatriate staff for the program.

Analysis of the ICRC's Impact on the Violence in Burundi

The impact of this type of program is impossible to evaluate. The results, if any, will be visible only in the long term. One Burundi woman expressed the dilemma as follows:

> In the course of the work I have sometimes been asked: "Look at the problems we have here in Burundi. Don't you think this work is an illusion?" I have answered: "Explaining to your children what is good

and bad is a long-term job, is it not? The message has to be repeated
again and again. You give birth, and you educate. You keep on. That is
the only way to change anything. We are building for the future. For
the time being it might be difficult to achieve anything, but you have
to start somewhere. We have started."

The political instability in Burundi has continued for years, with
frequent violence and killings. The country, however, has not experienced a full civil war (as has sometimes been predicted). It would seem,
therefore, that although some people in the society have an interest in
fomenting intergroup conflict, others are resistant to open warfare.
There are many stories of villages that have refused to follow the directions of "leaders" who have tried to incite them to violence.

In this situation, with pressures in both directions, an international
aid program can become part of the struggle. The ICRC dealt with this
possibility directly. Its dissemination program in Burundi provided
space and voice for antiviolence sentiments. The program was rooted in
the ICRC mandate, within which the ICRC creatively redesigned a standard program (dissemination) to lessen the likelihood of reinforcing
intergroup suspicions. That approach identified and reinforced existing capacities in Burundi that resist interethnic war.

The decision to organize a working group composed of local, respected, but "ordinary" (not well-known) individuals was a direct way to
support the Burundian basis for resistance to conflict manipulation.
And the decision to use Burundian sayings and proverbs, as well as traditional values and norms, increased the resonance of the message
among recipients.

Some Burundians, explaining why nationals have not been openly
involved in the village-level dissemination efforts, noted that the Declaration's message is better heard and better believed when it is delivered
by outsiders. Burundians would be seen as belonging to one group or
the other and, hence, as having a group-vested interest. The impartial-
ity and lack of group identity of the foreign staff of an international
agency allow people to hear the message for what it is—a neutral call to
reason within the Burundian context.

As the working group met to write the Declaration, it struggled with
the decision of how explicitly to name the crimes that had occurred in
Burundi. Some members were concerned that references to real events
could stir up emotions and thus incite reprisals. Others felt the message
could be carried only by dealing directly and honestly with the realities.
After much thought, everyone agreed it was important to name the reality, and the group focused on how to do so in ways that would encourage resistance to future violence.

This dilemma is frequently encountered by international agencies working in conflict situations. To what extent do attempts to address conflict end up by feeding into rather than mitigating it? The fact that the ICRC brought local people from many segments of Burundian society together and that they discussed the issue increased the probability that the decision taken would be appropriate in that setting. Furthermore, the working group's sense that it could avoid the potential negative impacts of telling the truth if it was careful in how it did so is important. A well-chosen group of local people who are genuinely interested in not exacerbating conflict can often better express things than an outside group can. A number of people interviewed for this case study commented that the ICRC is one of the few organizations that found a way to make Burundians listen. They judge the impact of the program to be strong and lasting.

10

The Harmony Project: Peace Building Amid Poverty in India

A Project of the Saint Xavier's Social Service Society in Ahmedabad, India

Ahmedabad is the largest city and the state capital of Gujurat on the northwest coast of India. During British rule the city was known as the "Manchester of India" because of its concentration on textile production, which remains significant today. Ahmedabad holds a special place in the history of India's independence movement because it was the base from which Mahatma Gandhi launched his historic march protesting the British Salt Law in 1915. Yet in spite of its identity with a preeminent nonviolent leader, Ahmedabad has also been the site of repeated, sometimes violent intercommunal rioting.

The region and the city suffer from periodic droughts and floods. Following a particularly severe flood of the Sabarmati River in the early 1970s, the Jesuit community of Catholic priests in Ahmedabad initiated the Saint Xavier's Social Service Society (hereafter the Society) to provide relief assistance to slum dwellers whose homes had been damaged. When the immediate emergency had passed, the Society continued and expanded its programs in Ahmedabad's slums, undertaking community organization and other development-oriented social service activities. As a result, when rioting broke out between Hindus and Muslims in the areas in which it worked, the Society staff felt committed and was in a position to respond.

This case study was written by Joseph Bock for the Local Charities for Peace Project with support from the Kellogg National Fellowship Program of the W. K. Kellogg Foundation and from Catholic Relief Services. It has been adapted and edited for this volume by Mary B. Anderson.

The Context of Violence

About 70 percent of Ahmedabad's population is Hindu, and 20 percent is Muslim. Rioting in the slums between these groups almost always occurs along sectarian lines.

Forty-one percent of Ahmedabad's population lives in what the municipal government estimates to be 1,023 slums. Many of the inhabitants migrated to Ahmedabad from rural parts of Gujarat when population pressure, poor harvests, or both resulted in food insecurity. Many are squatters who live on land that is not legally theirs or who rent from slumlords. Most build their own shacks using scavenged scraps of lumber, metal, and plastic. Crowding is a problem because of continual population growth and in-migration. An average family dwelling is 10 feet by 12 feet. Most slum areas lack sewage and storm water drainage facilities, although some have access to a shared water source.

Slum families usually earn their income (which averages U.S.$40 to $50 per month) as manual laborers, domestic workers, petty retailers, or semiskilled trade workers. Inflation in recent years has put enormous pressure on people's ability to make ends meet. Temperatures reach as high as 115 degrees Fahrenheit during four months of the year, so the heat inside the tin-roofed homes compels people to sleep in the filthy alleyways between houses. During the three-month monsoon, ankle-deep water is common; during high winds, the shacks sometimes collapse. In general, health is poorer and infant mortality is higher than in other parts of the city. Nonetheless, many slum dwellers are better off than they would have been had they stayed in the countryside.[1]

Politically, Gujarat state has been a stronghold of the Indian National Congress Party and one of its derivatives, the Congress (I) Party.[2] From the time of the first free elections in India in 1952 up to 1967, the Indian National Congress Party dominated in most parts of the country. In 1967, in a transition from a single party to a multiparty system, the Congress Party split and the Congress (I) Party emerged as the largest "descendent" party (so named because of Indira Gandhi's prominent role in the formation of the party).

In November 1989 the party suffered a major setback when the pro-Hindu Bharatiya Janata Party (BJP) gained significant political victories in several important locales, including the Ahmedabad municipal government. By 1998 the BJP had consolidated its regional successes into a national electoral victory and now dominated national politics.

The BJP political rhetoric has tended to highlight sectarian identities and thus to exacerbate interfaith tensions. Sometimes the result has been intersectarian riots.[3] The Congress (I) Party, on the other hand, is viewed as advocating a secular state. This party has been supported mainly by Muslims and low-income Hindus.

Interfaith Conflict

The factors leading to interfaith tensions in India have historical, economic, and psychological dimensions. Historical antecedents include repeated Muslim invasions that sometimes destroyed Hindu temples, militant proselytizing of Hindus by Muslims, a British colonial policy of divide and rule that pitted followers of the two faiths against each other, and the subsequent violent division of India and Pakistan along sectarian lines. Pakistan's existence as a separate homeland for Muslims provides an international forum that reinforces domestic intergroup distrust and tensions.

Economically, Hindus have tended to enjoy a higher standard of living and more and better job opportunities than Muslims. Competition for both government and private-sector jobs has often been interpreted in terms of competition between Hindus and Muslims. Psychologically, the groups' different theologies (Muslims are monotheistic whereas Hindus are polytheistic) are thought by some also to produce different worldviews.[4]

Interfaith rioting in Ahmedabad has been concentrated in the slums, where illiteracy is high and incomes are low. In these regions rumor and propaganda about the "other group" have been found to have potent effects on people's emotions and actions.

At times, riots have been severe. In 1969, for example, it is estimated that nearly 1,000 people died in riots in Ahmedabad.[5] Major riots occurred during November–December 1990 and December 1992 following the destruction of the mosque at Ayodhya by Hindu militants. Rioters throw stones, loot, and destroy homes and shops; some have also hurled burning rags into crowds. Men are responsible for most of the violence—especially murder—but women also participate, often attacking other women and children; women are also frequently involved in looting.

Many believe rioting in Ahmedabad is cultivated by some political leaders and real estate developers; others feel riots are triggered by organized militant groups with foreign support. For example, it is widely accepted that BJP leaders have engineered riots between Muslims and Hindus to solidify their political base and make the Congress (I) Party appear weak and ineffectual. BJP operatives have allegedly hired "gangsters"— some of whom are slum dwellers themselves—to foment religious violence during volatile periods. This has occurred mostly during religious holidays when sectarian collective identity is intensely defined and passions can be excited over the meaning of the event being celebrated.

When squatters live on land that has become commercially valuable, some real estate developers have used intergroup violence to terrify occupants so they flee to other locations. In a number of instances when slum dwellers have vacated an area because of a riot, their shacks have been leveled and the areas turned into more lucrative middle-class neighborhoods.

Women and children are often enlisted as propagandists by the people who engineer riots. Sometimes those who wish to promote intergroup violence print leaflets containing rumors intended to provoke mistrust and tensions and hire illiterate women or children to distribute them. Because they cannot read the message they are handing out, the women and children have no way to anticipate the impact of their leafleting. Political operatives also hang huge posters or paint slogans on walls in the slums that contain inflammatory messages, referring to the "other community" and accusing it of having acted against "our country." Sometimes these messages urge people not to patronize "their" shops or have other interactions with "them."

The Program of Saint Xavier's Social Service Society

As noted earlier Saint Xavier's Social Service Society began its work in the Ahmedabad slums following severe flooding in the early 1970s. From this base of emergency relief work, the Jesuit initiative has become involved in a number of slum neighborhoods. By the 1990s it was providing programs in community health, education, human rights, the environment, and women in development, as well as relief assistance when floods or riots occurred.

The Society is funded entirely by foreign donors, including Catholic agencies in Germany, Luxembourg, the Netherlands, Spain, Sweden, and the United States. The government of Switzerland also supports its work. Of the international NGOs that support the Society, Catholic Relief Services (CRS) is unique because it has field offices in India and provides U.S. government food commodities as well as cash grants. The Society, serving in a counterpart role to the CRS, provides food aid to a network of forty-eight partners in rural areas throughout Gujarat. The food program is important within the Society's relief and development activities. Much of the food is used in ongoing food for work activities in the countryside around Ahmedabad, and some is distributed in response to emergencies inside the city. The value of food commodities distributed annually by the Society is about U.S.$1 million.

Excluding the value of food, the Society's annual budget is only U.S.$30,000 to $40,000. Of that, just over half is devoted to work in the slums; the remainder covers salaries, rents, and the costs of a documentation center for social, environmental, health, and human rights issues. The professional staff includes twenty full-time people and numerous part-time workers, especially health care workers. Hindus, Muslims, Sikhs, Jains, and Christians work together on the staff. Those involved in slum work are Hindu and Muslim except for the Society's director, who is a Jesuit priest.

The Society works in the poorest communities of Ahmedabad, focusing on three major flood-prone areas. One, the Sankalitnagar slum where the Society began its work in 1973, has a population of nearly 25,000 people. Prior to the riots in 1991, this area was 60 percent Muslim and 40 percent Hindu. Since the riots only about 1 percent of the population is Hindu.

Another area in which the Society has worked since 1983, the Mahajan-no-Vando slum, has about 12,000 people living in a geographical area of 12,807 square meters. The slum is almost entirely Hindu, with only a few Muslim families living on the periphery. Many of those who live there depend on the Muslims to hire them for petty domestic jobs and on their shops for needed goods.

The third area, the Nagori Kabarasthan slum, where the Society also began work in 1983, is populated by about 18,000 people in an area of 10,556 square meters. Ninety-five percent of the residents are Hindu, with a few Muslim families both in the middle of the area and at the edges.

Beginning in 1992 the Society began an outreach program to twenty other slums in Ahmedabad. Most of these areas had at one time received emergency assistance from the Society after either a flood or a riot. Over the years the Society has helped the government to assess personal injuries and property damage in postriot areas, and it has provided medical care, food, and blankets to people who have suffered. In some cases the Society has helped to maintain temporary relief camps when people have been displaced, and it has provided financial support to help families purchase lumber and other materials to rebuild their destroyed homes. Such activities have not been limited to the areas in which the Society has ongoing programs. If a riot occurs, staff members are sent to the area to identify riot-related needs and provide assistance for a brief time.

The Society's main program focus is on community health. Activities include monitoring children's growth; providing health education, immunizations, midwifery training, and tuberculosis treatment; and when epidemics break out monitoring health outreach and effectiveness. Education programs focused at first on informal education intended to promote parents' awareness of the value of education. Activities included field trips, films, and educational and leadership camps for children. In recent years the program has moved toward encouraging children to attend formal schools. The Society's Human Rights Programme is aimed at increasing slum dwellers' awareness of their legal rights, particularly how to avoid being evicted from their houses. The program also focuses on the prevention of spousal abuse and educates women about their rights. Women's programming includes a savings program and maternal-child health care.

A Program to Cultivate Interfaith Harmony

A Jesuit priest and a native of India who was born in Bombay, the Society's director has committed himself to the "service of faith and promotion of justice." He respects all faiths but observes that "religion and religious beliefs are the most blinding of all passions, especially where the poor are concerned." He eschews violence and believes there is no theological basis in any religion for advocating violence over peace. As a result, he says his "heart aches" for anyone involved in violence—perpetrators as well as victims. These attitudes define his work in the Society and, to a large extent, the Society's programmatic approaches to interfaith rioting.

Safe havens.   Soon after its founding in the early 1970s, the Society began attempts to allay interfaith violence by providing a safe haven for a besieged minority of Muslims who were being attacked by a mob of Hindus. A church-affiliated school was opened to the Muslims, and the Society's staff negotiated with the mob to end their pursuit. The Society's director felt that in this situation it was an advantage to be a Christian because he was not identified with, or perceived to be biased toward, either side. On some occasions since this experience, the Society has again opened its own and other church-related buildings to provide a safe haven for groups under attack.

Myth busting.   The Society has engaged in myth busting in the slums. Aware of the power of rumors and propaganda to incite violence in these communities, Society staff members have adopted strategies to counteract false information and to educate people about how the manipulation of their emotions harms them and causes others (politicians and land developers) to gain.

For example, after an India-Pakistan cricket match a series of pamphlets appeared that "accused" neighborhood Muslims of "cheering for Pakistan." Society staff members quickly visited the community and asked, Have you seen any Muslims cheering, or if Pakistan made a good stroke, why can't you applaud it? This face-to-face engagement is intended to evoke more thoughtful responses, based on reality, from people who might otherwise be aroused into mob reactions. The Society director noted, the strategy is designed "to counter false propaganda as soon as it takes off—bit by bit and point by point." Sometimes this is done on the streets; sometimes a community meeting is called.

Street plays.   Whereas providing a safe haven and undertaking rumor-countering campaigns are actions that attempt to preempt violence after problems have emerged, the Society has also adopted strategies to keep people from being provoked into violence. In 1991, in response to the riots in late 1990, the Society hired a consultant to work with the staff to write a street play that was performed throughout the area. The response was so positive that street plays became a regular programmatic activity of the Society.

The play writing began as a collective effort. Staff members divided into groups, and each group presented a different version of an agreed story. A composite script was then written that took the best ideas from each improvisational presentation. Slum dwellers later became involved in writing and performing in the plays.

Plays have been tailored to local situations. They depict events that are relevant and familiar to viewers on the streets, and they use common symbols and words. As events change, new information and symbolism are added. Some plays dramatize the etiology of riots, unfolding the processes by which land developers or politicians use local people or gangsters to stir up emotions through rumor. All of the plays are designed to counteract emotional appeals for violence with rational, locally relevant arguments against violence. They present different ways people can behave when tensions rise. Through frequent performances—reported to be more popular than television among many slum dwellers—the plays are meant to keep the message of intercommunal harmony before the people.

Competitions.   The Society has sponsored art competitions on the theme of interfaith harmony among slum children. Children are given paper and colored markers. The program is seen as another way to raise awareness of sectarian violence in a manner that is fun and rewarding for children. Interest and participation have increased regularly, and the Society has expanded its competitions to include essay, poetry, and poster-making contests for high school–age children.

People's festivals.   Once a year the Society collaborates with other local organizations to sponsor a People's Festival, which usually includes a community meal. In 1993 "harmony" was chosen as the festival theme, and everyone who attended was given a plastic bag with snacks. On the plastic bags were the words to a song the Society's staff had written that was performed at the festival. The tune was catchy, and it immediately caught on. The song was sung and the plastic bags were reused for many months afterward. An English translation of the song goes:

> Here is the message of communal harmony:
> Allah and Ishwar are one.
> Do not fight over a temple or mosque;
> Politicians fight for power.
> The huts of the poor are set aflame:
> The lust for power is the fuel.
> Look at what has happened to our city!
> For someone's fault, someone else is punished.
> If we, the people, live in harmony
> Nobody will dare to disunite us.
> This is the message of communal harmony.

Peace committees.   The most important aspect of the Society's programming involves encouraging the formation of local peace committees among slum dwellers. The Society's health, education, women's, and environmental programs all involve local committees. Within and around this formal structure, slum dwellers have established other informal committees for a variety of purposes.

Following the riots in 1992, the Society began to support and encourage the establishment of informal peace committees in affected areas. These committees provide a forum for the expression of tensions before they escalate and constitute a place from which to launch collective action to avert violence. They provide a direct link between the Society's development and relief programs and its preventive and preemptive peace activities.

These committees have had some success. On one occasion a group of Hindus approached a slum that had an active peace committee, intending to attack Muslim residents. The Hindus who lived in the area met the attackers and said "you must kill us first." The attackers disbanded. The local peace committee organized this response.

In another location majority Hindus helped minority Muslims by bringing them food and water when the government imposed a curfew in anticipation of a riot. Personal relationships have been developed and nurtured through these harmony promotion efforts. When communal passions were running high in one area, Hindus sat on the steps of Muslim homes to prevent Hindu violence against the residents.

Analysis of the Program

The Society's harmony promotion activities represent an addition to the original programming. As has been the case for many relief and development agencies, circumstances erupted around the Society's programs that directly affected staff members' ability to do their jobs. When riots occurred in program areas, ongoing work was disrupted; when riots occurred in other areas, staff members were called on to respond, which also affected ongoing work. It was impossible to avoid some kind of riot response program.

Although staff members can cite many instances in which their work has made a positive difference in averting violence, overall the harmony promotion programs have been insufficient to prevent violence between the two religious groups. Rioting and interfaith fighting continue, and Society staff and workers have at times been threatened and targeted by promoters of violence and by mobs. Staff members feel differently about the appropriateness of their involvement in promoting harmony. Whereas some are committed to this role, others are less so. In some instances when tensions have run high, Society staff members have merged into crowds or found ways to escape rather than assume a leadership role (which may or may not have had any positive effect). The depth of intergroup suspicion and mistrust, regularly fed and cultivated by some interests, can create circumstances in which small efforts by brave individuals are apparently ineffectual. The Society's director and staff, as well as the peace committees, are constantly challenged to find ever more effective and extensive strategies to stop the interfaith violence in the communities where they live and work.

Future Strategies

Some of the programs tried so far suggest future strategies that could become increasingly effective.

Using relief and development programs to reinforce harmony promotion activities.   Society staff members strongly believe their ongoing relief and development programs lend legitimacy and credibility to the additional peace promotion activities they undertake. Without this program base in the community, they feel they could not undertake any of the activities designed to create intergroup harmony.

The synergism between the Society's development and relief work and its promotion of interfaith harmony suggests possible additional programming options. Because they have built trust within the communities through their daily programming, Society staff members are able to address sensitive issues in intergroup relationships. The Society has also identified opportunities to use regular programming inputs to link Muslims and Hindus around common interests such as schooling for children or public health projects. The agency has also brought people together around common concerns by hiring them as staff members and workers. An ongoing challenge is to develop other programs that highlight and make functional the two groups' interdependence without necessarily stating explicitly the goal of intergroup harmony.

Combining and overlapping strategies to promote harmony.   The Society has also been creative in developing a range of harmony support program approaches, including those focused on preventing intergroup mistrust and those focused on preempting likely violence when tensions arise. Staff members recognize that no single tactic alone can be effective.

Again, as it continues to expand its outreach in slum communities, the Society is challenged to capitalize on the cumulative effects of multiple small, locally based activities. The annual People's Festival provides one opportunity to showcase the many actions different subcommunities have undertaken and thereby reinforce their impacts. Finding other ways to link and thus to enlarge the activities of groups within and across slum areas (when adjacent slums are populated by different religious groups) poses a continuing programming challenge.

Differentiating religious identities from religious symbols.   Society staff members understand the difference between identity and symbols. They have seen that some violence occurs between groups with different religious identities but around issues that are nonreligious, whereas in other instances violence is focused specifically on religious symbols. In general, the strategies they have employed to avert violence seem to have been more successful in the former cases than in the latter. When rioting involves the destruction of a temple or a mosque, the symbolic importance of these structures raises emotions that are the most difficult to control.

Increasingly, the Society is undertaking programs that involve "manipulation inoculation"—that is, education about who gains (land developers and politicians) and who loses (the people who live in the slums) from interfaith violence. If enough people are involved in the analysis of the ways violence hurts them, the expectation (and hope) is that they will be less affected by the rumors and propaganda techniques employed by riot instigators.

Finding solutions to problems at the level of the problem.   The Society has focused on promoting harmony at the community level where intergroup violence occurs. Programs aimed at addressing violence are focused on the places where the violence occurs.

Some of the sources of the problems that lead to rioting lie outside the communities, so other programming options might be suggested. If outsiders routinely foment violence, is there a way the Society (and its partner agencies) could address those sources of tension more directly? Alternatively, what can those in the slums (with the support of the Society) do to insulate themselves from external influences that result in internal destruction? Are there ways the Society can use its increasing national reputation for excellent programming and possibly its international linkages to raise larger social issues that if addressed could reduce the likelihood that slum dwellers would easily resort to violence?

Conclusion

The Society is small, and the problems of the Ahmedabad slums are large. It would be unreasonable to suggest that the Society's programs alone could end interfaith violence in that part of India. In the locations in which they work and as they go about their daily activities, however, the staff members of this agency are finding ways to address the very real problems of intergroup rioting through direct programming and—possibly even more useful in the long run—through integrating activities that link the two religious communities in the regular, ongoing relief and development programs that constitute the Society's work.

11

Village Rehabilitation: Supporting Local Rebuilding in Somalia

A Project of Trocaire in Gedo, Somalia

In September 1992, at the height of the famine and war in Somalia, many Western agencies were faced with a difficult decision. Should they intervene in a country in which the need was enormous but where they had no prior experience and no local partners, or must they sit and watch as the famine worsened and more and more people died?

Among the many NGOs that decided to intervene was a small, twenty-one-year-old Irish agency named Trocaire,[1] the relief and development agency of the Catholic Church in Ireland. Until 1992 the agency had provided funding and technical assistance to indigenous NGOs in developing countries. Trocaire saw its mandate as promoting long-term development by building up the capacities of local people; it had never considered dispatching expatriates to work in a developing country. Somalia was the first instance in which the agency felt that with the apparent dearth of locally organized effort during the critical stages of famine, the only alternative was to initiate its own operations on the ground. This it did with a multisectoral relief and rehabilitation program based in the Gedo region in southwestern Somalia, one of the areas most seriously affected by the famine.

This case was originally researched and written by Stephen Jackson in 1995. It has been edited and amended by Mary B. Anderson for inclusion in this volume.

The Context of the War and the Famine

The broad facts of the Somalia war and famine are well-known.[2] From 1969 (nine years after Somalia achieved independence from England and Italy) to 1991, Major General Mohamed Siad Barre ruled Somalia. His one-party government, which espoused scientific socialism, maintained power through strong state control, manipulation of clan[3] interests, and appeals to claims on territories within the borders of neighboring states such as Kenya, Ethiopia, and Djibouti.

During much of Barre's regime, Somalia's fate was bound up in the superpower politics of the Cold War. First receiving substantial funding and military training from the Soviet Union and later, as circumstances and alliances in surrounding countries shifted, from the United States, the regime lasted longer than it likely would have without outsider influence. The regime's manipulation of clan identities, in turn, bred government instability that then required more manipulation. Throughout the 1980s Barre's regime was involved in all-out war and serious human rights abuses against the northern clans. By 1990 clan unrest had erupted across Somalia, and Barre was under attack from several fronts. The fronts formed a fragile coalition that finally unseated Barre (who fled to West Africa) in a bloody civil war in 1991.

The coalition lasted no longer than Barre's immediate ouster. Different clan families and interests emerged, causing the dissolution of the coalition as the groups competed for power. On the streets of Mogadishu, a fratricidal war broke out as two clans of the Hawiye clan family fought for control with little concern for the civilian population. Meanwhile, the northern part of the country declared unilateral independence under the name Somaliland, and the country's southwestern agricultural heartland was laid waste by successive troop movements through it. The local population, mostly small farmers historically despised by the more powerful nomadic pastoralist groups, were easy prey for the different factions. Fields were razed, grain stores pillaged, and people massacred. Farming was impossible, and the fields were not prepared for the rains.

By early 1992 a major disaster was clearly imminent, but the world media did not begin to report the awful events occurring in southern Somalia until early summer. By then, several hundred thousand people were at risk. Areas in the Bay and Gedo regions in the southwest experienced some of the highest rates of mortality recorded in modern times.[4]

The Gedo Region

The Gedo region lies at the southwestern extreme of Somalia, bordering Kenya and Ethiopia. Like much of the rest of the country, it is fairly dry. In the west, however, areas near two rivers are fertile and verdant, producing large amounts of agricultural produce during peacetime. In the dry lands, pastoralists are forced to migrate seasonally in search of water for their camel herds.

Along with the Bay region, Gedo was one of the areas of the country the most strongly affected by the 1992 war, in part because the area is home to the majority of the Marehan clan, the group from which Barre emerged and drew much of his political support. During Barre's regime Gedo had enjoyed considerable patronage and largesse from the central government. With his fall Gedo's favored position ended, and other clans that had resented Gedo's relative wealth took advantage of the warfare to loot and destroy the region. Many residents were chased from their homes or killed.

In addition, many people who fled the cruelties of war in other parts of Somalia—including the towns of Mogadishu, Baidoa, and Kismayo—made their way to Gedo. Some of the displaced persons were Marehan and were absorbed into existing villages; others had no prior connection to the area and formed new "villages" or crossed into Kenya and became refugees in the camps along the border. The population of Bulla Hawa, the main town in Gedo, increased from 5,000 to an estimated 50,000 people during this period. The population growth severely strained local resources.

During 1992 almost all agricultural activity ceased in Gedo. Camel herders were fortunate if they could keep their livestock during the fighting. They were often robbed or forced to kill or sell their animals for food. Crops in the river-fed agricultural regions were uprooted, and seed was contaminated or stolen. Pumps for drawing water for irrigation were a major target of looters, and many were lost.

Thus the normally small population of the Gedo region was overwhelmed by the arrival of many displaced people at the time when most of the usual agricultural activity had ceased and supply routes from ports had been cut by fighting. Large numbers of people clustered on the edges of villages in hastily assembled shelters or were concentrated in newly created villages in outlying areas. Famine and deaths from disease followed. To and fro fighting by warring factions for territorial control added to the sense of threat and instability. It was into this context that Trocaire arrived to launch its program.

The Trocaire Rehabilitation Program

Trocaire began its work in the Gedo region by distributing food and other emergency supplies in September 1992. By January 1993, however, its efforts had shifted to reconstructing for the future through rehabilitation programs in agriculture, health, education, and water. By the end of 1994, veterinary and sanitation programs had been added. Between 1992 and 1994, Trocaire spent U.S.$4.5 million on its Gedo programs.

Trocaire's Entry into Somalia

Trocaire began to consider some form of intervention in Somalia in early 1992. The agency's traditional mandate of operating through indigenous NGOs, however, constrained it to seek out opportunities to provide relief assistance through local counterparts. Trocaire had no previous involvement in the country, so the search for counterparts took time. In the end, Trocaire was forced to conclude (as were many other agencies) that under the circumstances then existing in Somalia, no ready counterparts were available. The agency decided to send expatriates to work in Somalia.

Funding for the program was raised from a variety of sources. The Irish public had responded generously to the Somali crisis, particularly after a September visit to the region by Ireland's president, Mary Robinson. Public donations provided the basis for the early efforts. Funds also came from the Irish government, from other agencies within the wider Catholic relief and development network, and from the United Nations and bilateral donors. Some of Trocaire's later operational flexibility on the ground was the result of its wide funding base at this early stage, with much of the money untied to specific activities.

One of Trocaire's emergency officers and the agency's deputy director traveled to Somalia in early September 1992. They decided to base operations in the Gedo region because of the horrific conditions in the region and in the refugee camps just over the Kenyan border. A further factor in their choice was that many other international agencies were locating in the town of Baidoa in the neighboring Bay region.

Initially, emergency food deliveries were begun in cooperation with the International Committee of the Red Cross (ICRC), the United Nations High Commissioner for Refugees (UNHCR), and Catholic Relief Services (CRS). A small early seed distribution was conducted in river areas to try to restart agricultural production. Some early work was also done in the refugee camp that had formed unofficially in Mandera, Kenya. The security situation was so precarious in Somalia, however, that its obvious greater need caused Trocaire to focus its program on Gedo.

Important Early Decisions

In the first days and months of operation, Trocaire made several important decisions about its work in Somalia that continued to shape its programming choices and the impact its programs had on the conflict.

Within a few months of startup, Trocaire decided to end its emergency work and to focus instead on rebuilding for the future. Thus the agency ended the food distribution program, and it did so in a way that built toward and reinforced its development orientation.

Trocaire staff members consulted with local groups to minimize the potential harmful effects of the decision to terminate food aid so early. Staff members traveled through the region and met with elders to explain why food aid was being cut. First, they had to allay suspicions that the termination was a prelude to a complete withdrawal of aid from the area. Second, they had to communicate that food aid was being discontinued in all areas at the same time so there would be no perception of unequal treatment. Third and perhaps most important, staff members held lengthy discussions with communities about why the program was ending. Discussion focused on the dangers of fostering dependency and depressing local agricultural production; the intent to spend program money on sustainable ends that would continue to benefit Gedo long after Trocaire's departure; and the waning of international attention on Somalia, which meant that a supply of relief food could not be guaranteed forever. The underlying message was that Trocaire was always willing to listen to community interests.

This approach—that it was worth the time to discuss ideas and decisions with the people who would be affected—established the tone and mode of Trocaire's work even as the crisis proceeded. The approach later became one of the pillars of Trocaire's programming, its Community Awareness Program (CAP).

From the beginning, Trocaire staff members were aware of the need to base their work in the community structures that were being reestablished after the recent destruction. They also recognized the urgent need to address directly the divisive effects of the extremist clanism that had increased during both the Barre regime and the civil war that followed. To meet these needs, the Trocaire staff recommended a pedagogic approach for working with Somali communities to build a sense of unity and purpose and to overcome expatriate suspicion of Somali workers and Somali susceptibility to clanism. The methodology would be used both within the Trocaire staff and subsequently with clan elders in the communities.

The Development Education Leadership Teams in Action (DELTA) methodology, developed in Kenya over a fifteen-year period by the development arm of the Kenyan Catholic Church, was chosen for application in Somalia. The DELTA approach is derived from the development theology and pedagogy of Brazilian Paolo Freire, known by his term *conscientization*.[5] The pedagogy, in Freire's words, is "forged *with* and not *for*" (his emphasis) the people it serves. DELTA trainers were brought from Kenya to work with local and expatriate staff. Subsequent local staff members were trained in the approach and used it in villages as they carried out the Community Awareness Program (CAP).

CAP fostered relations and communication between Trocaire and the communities being served. CAP staff members visited villages, established ongoing relations with village members, conducted workshops on development and community participation, and published a monthly newsletter in both Somali and English.

Another early decision was equally, if not more important in establishing Trocaire's message and tone in Gedo: the principled decision not to use armed guards to protect Trocaire's staff or goods. The Somali "technicals"—Toyota pickup trucks or Landcruisers turned into battlewagons with heavy artillery or machine guns welded to their structures—became the international media's favorite image for portraying the conflict, which helped to create the appearance of an insecure situation for NGOs working in the country. By late 1992 throughout the south agencies were employing gunmen to accompany relief convoys and workers. Cars with gunmen were hired as part of a "package." NGO compounds were guarded by teams armed with AK-47s and other assault weapons acquired during the Cold War years.

Trocaire was one of very few agencies to decide not to join the militarized economy of Somalia.[6] The decision was not easy to reach since the region in which Trocaire operated was highly contested. In spite of some potential danger and occasional threats of violence, Trocaire took this decision because it believed building bridges with local structures would support the agency's safety and, more fundamentally, help the communities.

Trocaire also made an early decision to limit the number of expatriate staff; there were never more than five internationals in the Gedo regional program. Staff members were drawn mostly from the local refugee and displaced populations, within which were individuals with considerable technical skill and some managerial experience. As word circulated that Trocaire was interested in filling positions, many people expressed interest. A number of those selected were referred by individuals already hired. Although some concern was expressed that such a strategy would lead to a concentration of jobs within one clan or family, that did not happen. The eventual staff team was broadly representative, in part because it was selected on the basis of academic background and work experience.

Coordinators for the first four programming sectors—agriculture, water, health, and education—were found quickly. They included two doctors, one hydrogeologist, one educator, and one political scientist.

Ten months after the beginning of the program, Trocaire began to transfer management and control to Somali staff. A Somali management team was selected by and from among the local staff to take control of operations. Some expatriate staff members felt this development came too early because of a perceived lack of preparedness of the Somalis to deal with demands for "assistance" from villages in which the Somalis had relatives or other close connections. As a result of extraneous timing issues that affected the larger agency, some managerial control was later reclaimed by Trocaire headquarters. The precedent had clearly been set, however, and the Somali program was ultimately owned by Somalis.

Although Trocaire phased out its work in the Mandera refugee camp very early, it retained an administrative operational base there. This base provided a degree of insulation from immediate physical threats by Somali factions and deemphasized the administrative functions of the Bulla Hawa (Somalia) office. Much staff discussion and disagreement occurred over the importance of basing a Somali program within Somalia. In one instance after more administrative functions had been moved to Bulla Hawa, however, personnel there were attacked. Thus the decision was made to maintain two locations to avoid some of the control and possible misuse of resources local warring factions often force on agencies operating in their areas.

Early Outcomes

As this case study was written, Trocaire's program in the Gedo region had been in operation for about two years and was still very active. In consultation with local staff members and village elders in the northern half of Gedo, operational plans had been drawn up that covered everything from reestablishing agricultural productivity in river-fed areas to sinking boreholes to reopening the school system. Many of these activities were under way and had experienced some success.

For example, by October 1994 Trocaire had (re)opened eighteen schools in northern Gedo. This represented a considerable increase over prewar educational conditions, so the achievement presented problems as well as successes. By providing maximum possible access to education, the program had gone beyond local communities' capabilities to sustain this number of schools in the long run. Recognizing this problem, the staff shifted its attention from providing schools to building a sustainable system of management for existing schools. This involved setting up town or village education committees made up of one elder, a headmaster or headmistress, two parents, and one CAP member. The result has been a forum in which people who share a common interest (education) have come together to discuss issues and solve problems (of sustaining the programs). In the "new" postwar villages where displaced people live, the education committees include people from the various clans.

The decision not to hire armed guards has had a significant effect on Trocaire's ability to carry out programs with communities in the area. At first, Trocaire staff members made it clear to village elders that they would not pay for security. People in the area knew from other parts of Somalia that money could be made by providing security for agencies, but there had been few precedents in Gedo. Faced with the direct choice offered by Trocaire—aid and no demands for gun money or no aid (or, if such demands came later, withdrawal of aid)—villages chose the former. Elders accepted responsibility for controlling threats and attempts to extort.

Another factor that made it easier to avoid the use of guns was the (then) increasing presence in Gedo of Islamic *fundamentalists*.[7] These groups were noted for their honesty and propriety and had a stabilizing effect in the areas in which they were strong.

Many local people explained Trocaire's ability to remain unarmed as a result of "clan unity" in Gedo. They claimed loyalty to the Marehan clan is so strong that armed protection in areas in which the clan predominates is unnecessary. The experience of other agencies and even occasionally of Trocaire, however, has seemed to challenge the accuracy of this explanation.

On the negative side, Trocaire's refusal to hire guards created considerable resentment among some Somalis who might have gained from security contracts. Such individuals tried early on to scare Trocaire staff members into hiring guards by threatening them. The staff resisted this pressure because of the earlier decision to maintain an administrative office across the border in Kenya. If threats became too great, the staff members would tell local communities that they would withdraw to Kenya until their safety could be assured in Somalia.

In general, the elders' agreements to guarantee Trocaire's safety held. Some felt this reliance on the elders strengthened their ability to keep warring factions in check and gave them some bargaining leverage over militia groups.

In May 1994, however, when a community grievance threatened to become violent, Trocaire was forced to close its operations for one month and move across the border into Kenya. The World Food Program (WFP) had resumed Food for Work programs in much of Gedo. Aware that Trocaire had conducted similar activities in Bulla Hawa in late 1992, the WFP organized its new program in all areas of Gedo except Bulla Hawa (apparently presuming Trocaire would make decisions for that area).

When the town's omission from the WFP program became known to its residents, they assumed Trocaire had prevented the WFP from coming into Bulla Hawa. The rumor gained ground quickly, and anger toward Trocaire grew. Demonstrations against the agency were organized, and Trocaire's vehicles were stoned as they passed through town.

Trocaire's reaction was immediate. All operations were suspended, and a meeting was sought with town elders. As the grievance was finally aired and Trocaire understood the cause of the anger, the agency assured the elders that it claimed no territorial rights over Gedo and would never interfere with the operations of any other agency that wanted to work there. The staff also conveyed the message that if misunderstandings ever arose again, violent threats would not be tolerated, and Trocaire would consider total withdrawal.

Since in response to the crisis Trocaire suspended all of its activities in Gedo and not just those in Bulla Hawa, other parts of the region put pressure on the town's elders to come to agreement with the agency sooner rather than later. Considerable recriminations were laid at Bulla Hawa's door for interrupting the flow of assistance by its "excessive greed" for the "spoils" of a Food for Work program. Trocaire returned to full operations, and a liaison "committee of eight" was established by the elders to handle any future dealings on such matters.[8]

Analysis of Trocaire's Program

The Trocaire experience in the Gedo region of Somalia from 1992 through 1994 highlights two important points. First, this case demonstrates that an agency's earliest programming decisions as it begins its work are critically important for subsequent relations with both the communities in which it works and the impacts of its inputs. Although Trocaire's decision to rely heavily on local staff and to work through community structures was in part reflective of its ambivalence toward becoming operational, it nonetheless put pressure on the first expatriate staff members in the field to find qualified local people to take over quickly. The decision also set the terms—with full support from headquarters—to take time to travel extensively, stay in communities, talk with lots of people, and reflect on what was said.

The necessity to respond to urgent needs was met through an immediate food distribution program, but the agency's heart was not in that program for the long term. The life-saving activities were undertaken to save lives, of course, but also to lay the groundwork for a shift to a longer-term focus as early as possible. Trocaire was able to shift its focus early in part because other agencies continued to provide food to the area. Rather than continuing to be the conduit for food distributions, Trocaire put its own resources (staff time and funds) into rehabilitation and future-oriented activities.

The manner in which the shift was made was probably as important as the shift itself. Extensive consultations with communities prior to disbanding the feeding program allayed local fears of abandonment and conveyed the message that Trocaire respected the people and wanted to maintain a relationship of trust with them. And ensuring that everyone knew they would all receive the same treatment achieved a transparency of action that seemed important in the context of conflict in which intergroup suspicions abound.

A lesson can be taken from this experience: Clear communication with recipients about decisions to end certain program activities can help to convey respect and maintain trust. It also seems that careful thought before beginning consultations is important. What should be said and how, likely reactions and agency responses, and clarification of areas in which compromise is or is not possible—should all be well thought through before staff venture out into the field.

Furthermore, the end of a program activity seems to offer a particular opportunity to convey messages that can be especially important in war areas. Messages of trust and mutual respect have been named; additionally, such consultation conveys the importance of communities rebuilding themselves and taking back responsibility for future basic needs and distributional systems and for dealing with shortages. These responsibilities require community interaction and some level of joint decisionmaking—necessary steps in moving away from conflict and toward a normal community life.

The second lesson the Trocaire case highlights is the importance of the implicit messages programming approaches convey to recipient communities. Decisions to work primarily through existing local structures; to maintain a high degree of transparency in all dealings; to hire, trust, and turn over operations to local staff; to establish systems for protection that did not rely on arms; and to move toward future-oriented programming at the earliest possible moment not only shaped Trocaire's programs but also conveyed implicit messages to local people.

Working through local structures always risks reinforcing the power of destructive or self-interested systems at the expense of the majority of the people. However, Trocaire seemed to avoid this through the breadth of its consultations. Staff members traveled widely, consulted with many people on many occasions, and did so transparently so everyone knew who else was consulted.

Trusting local staff in the context of war can also reinforce local power blocks and ultimately exclude some groups and favor others. Trocaire seemed to avoid this through its explicit qualifications for employment (academic background and previous work experience). In this context these qualifications were spread sufficiently broadly among clan groups that the pool of people who could be hired was not limited to single families. (In some settings, if educational opportunity or employment patterns consistently favor one group over others, such a strategy could reinforce privilege and feed intergroup competition.)

Because its approach resulted in a broadly mixed staff, Trocaire's hiring policies carried several positive implicit messages. A dependence on local staff conveys the sense that this country can and will regain nonwar "normalcy" in which local people hold jobs and are responsible for decisions. Such dependence also communicates that even if problems among people arise, they can be sorted out without violence. Systems for working together can be reestablished. The mixing of clan groups to work on a common set of activities conveys a message of shared interests and concerns. The Community Awareness Program was staffed explicitly with people who represented various groups in society. Each team that visited villages included men and women, older and younger people, and individuals from different clans. The purpose was to mix them so they could reestablish working relations around common activities and also to be able to reach out effectively to different people in the communities.

The decision to move toward future-oriented programming also conveyed confidence in Somalis and in the country's future nonwar "normalcy." In the midst of civil war, the idea that the conflict will end and that people will be able to live normally again can have a powerful and welcome effect on local people. Program activities focused in this way also provide a forum in which people can act in nonwar ways.

Finally, the decision to base staff and program security in systems other than arms had direct impacts on the war and conveyed implicit messages to observers. We noted earlier that the decision may have reinforced the power of civilian leadership (elders) relative to that of military leadership. Furthermore, evidence clearly shows that payments to guards fed directly into Somalia's military economy. Avoiding such payments was one way to keep from directly supporting warriors and arms.

Interviews with local people indicated that the implicit message of this decision was also important. The decision reminded people that it was possible to be safe without arms. It reminded people that civilian structures can maintain order, and it reinforced the community's sense of responsibility for doing so. It supported the creation of committees (village education committees, the Bulla Hawa elders' liaison committee of eight) to address disagreements, misunderstandings, and problems when they arose through discussion (a deep tradition in Somalia) rather than through an immediate resort to threat.

Summary

The two-year span of this case study is insufficient to make broad judgments about Trocaire's impact on either the region's developmental prospects or the area's larger conflict and its conflictproneness. Some of the approaches taken, however, suggest programming alternatives and options that may have some positive effects in conflict contexts. Examples are suggested of ways to avoid worsening some aspects of warfare and of ways to use program mechanisms to reduce intergroup tensions and support nonwar capacities in a postconflict society. Although small and local, such examples raise the salient question of whether all aid agencies could try similar approaches and, if so, whether the cumulative effect could significantly help local people who want to do so to disengage from war.

PART THREE

Conclusion

12

Reflecting on the Role of Aid

When international assistance is given in the context of a violent conflict, it becomes a part of that context and thus also of the conflict. These are the words with which we began this book, and we return to them as we close. This much we know.

We also know a great deal about how aid and the context of conflict interact. The preceding pages have recorded experiences and ideas from aid workers and compiled them into patterns and formulations that can help future aid workers who face new challenges in conflict settings. A tool for pulling together these lessons in program design and implementation is offered in Chapter 6. Although as events unfold some of the individual examples cited may have impacts we have not anticipated (either negative or positive), our experience in compiling and reviewing them with many experienced colleagues gives us confidence that the essential lessons and ideas presented will prove useful over time.

We cannot close, however, without raising two additional concerns that deserve and require additional learning. They have challenged us from the beginning of this effort, and they continue to do so now.

The first is the issue of how the micro level of warfare (and peacefare) relates to the macro level. As we have indicated, the approach of the Local Capacities for Peace Project was inductive; it started with local and individualized experiences and accumulated many of those experiences into a larger picture. But this process has not bridged the gap between communities at war and the international context in which intranational wars occur. We know outside forces affect and sometimes perpetuate internal wars. Neighboring (and sometimes not so neighboring) countries pursue their interests through policies and direct subsidies of money, weapons, and even fighters.

Beyond this, the world's larger sociopolitical-economic arrangements also influence, shape, respond, or fail to respond to crises that occur within countries. This book has not examined the ways international assistance can and does directly interact with these macrolevel forces. Many have noted that humanitarian assistance should not be expected to substitute for the failed political will of nations that ignore violent crises in other countries. This point was saliently made in connection with the world's failed political response to the unfolding events of Rwanda's genocide.[1] But as a community, international aid agencies have not yet found the way to insist that appropriate political actions be taken while remaining nonpolitical in providing aid wherever it is needed.

Our findings here suggest that international aid may play a role in enabling people in a wartorn society to exert influence to gain the international political assistance they need and want. But much more is to be tried—and learned—in this area. This role has become and will continue to become increasingly important as international aid agencies and political forces interact in areas of unfolding violent crisis.

Second and related, more is to be learned about the appropriate relationship between outsiders and insiders in conflict areas. All aid workers know that even in peacetime, the role of outside aid providers, as foreigners, taking responsibility for other people's welfare is complicated and challenging. Civil wars are the most complex domestic (insider) situations. The ways outsiders enter and assume important roles in these circumstances correspondingly pose the most complex moral, as well as practical, challenges aid workers face.

We have argued here that aid workers should try to identify local capacities for peace and connectors and design their aid programs to support and reinforce them. Even as we have made this argument, however, we have asked ourselves: "Who do we think we are? Is it justified for outsiders to choose among people or institutions, to make judgments about who or what is 'truly' a local capacity for peace? To what extent might our attempts to do so constitute dangerous and inappropriate social engineering?"

We have found no easy answers to these questions. What we have found is an openness among our colleagues whose countries are in conflict to accept our involvement in their domestic problems—up to a point. That is, many people in warring societies invite outsider ideas and appreciate outsider analyses of what is going on within their communities. Such interventions are accepted for what they are—caring, arising from broad international experience, and definitely outsider. *Outsider*, in this sense, has both disadvantages (incomplete knowledge) and advantages (perspective, no identity with the sides in the conflict).

The fact that aid inevitably does have an impact on warfare means aid workers cannot avoid the responsibility of trying to shape that impact. The fact that choices about how to shape that impact represent outsider interference means aid workers can always be accused of inappropriate action. There is no way out of this dilemma.

Since the dilemma cannot be escaped, we must continue to explore and learn how best to play the outsider role. We feel certain it is better for aid to support nonwar attitudes and actions than to reinforce and exacerbate conflict. How this is best done in each setting, by different kinds of aid and different aid workers, requires further experience and reflection. Thus this book represents only a work in progress; there is always more to be learned. Reflecting on our own and our colleagues' experiences can provide new insights into ways to do the job better. The suffering and creativity of people who live in societies that experience pervasive violence provide the motivation for continuing to learn and improve.

Acronyms

BJP	Bharatiya Janata Party (India)
CAP	Community Awareness Program
CRS	Catholic Relief Services
DELTA	Development Education Leadership Teams in Action
DHA	Department of Humanitarian Affairs (UN)
FFW	Food for Work
ICRC	International Committee of the Red Cross
IDF	Israeli Defense Force
IDP	internally displaced person
IHL	International Humanitarian Law
INGO	international nongovernmental organization
LCPP	Local Capacities for Peace Project
LCPs	local capacities for peace (general)
MNF	multinational force
NGO	nongovernmental organization
OLS	Operation Lifeline Sudan
PLO	Palestine Liberation Organization
SCF	Save the Children Federation
UNHCR	United Nations High Commissioner for Refugees
UNICEF	United Nations Children's Fund
UNIFIL	United Nations Interim Force in Lebanon
UNRISD	United Nations Research Institute for Social Development
WFP	World Food Program

Notes

Chapter 1

1. Fifteen case studies were carried out in fourteen conflict zones. Subsequently, twenty-four feedback workshops, each involving between twenty and forty people, were held in field and headquarter locations of active agencies. Thus about a thousand individuals were directly involved in generating the project's ideas and findings.

Chapter 5

1. United States Mission to the United Nations, *Global Humanitarian Emergencies* (New York: April 1997), p. 14.

Chapter 7

1. Many people in Tajikistan provided help in the writing of this case study. Special appreciation goes to Kenny Gluck, director of the SCF program, who provided many of the critical insights included in the case.

2. Galia Golan, "Ethnicity and the Problems of Central Asia," paper prepared for Rand, December 1993 (unpublished), p. 18.

3. Ibid.

4. Ibid., p. 19.

5. Ibid., pp. 18–19.

6. Ibid., p. 20.

7. Ibid., pp. 20–21.

8. UNHCR documents.

9. The information reflected in this section comes from interviews with a number of district government personnel in various parts of Khatlon Province carried out in spring 1994 by Mary B. Anderson and Tim Brodhead.

10. The information in this section that describes SCF's programming comes from interviews with SCF staff members in Dushanbe and Khatlon and from the project proposal submitted by SCF's Commodity Assisted Development and Emergency Response Unit to USAID in March 1994 entitled "Project Description: Tajikistan Humanitarian Assistance Program for Khatlon Region for the Period April 1, 1994, to June 30, 1996."

11. This quotation and others in this section are taken directly from the SCF proposal for USAID funding.

Chapter 8

When he wrote the case, Greg Hansen acknowledged assistance of many people in UNICEF/Lebanon, including Amal Dibo, former *SAWA* project officer; Anna Mansour, former Education for Peace program officer; Andre Roberfroid, former UNICEF representative; Dario Loda, senior program officer; Aida Jamal, external relations officer; and the *SAWA* and Education for Peace teams for their kindness and valuable assistance.

1. Background information on the war is derived from Dilip Hiro, *Lebanon: Fire and Embers* (New York: St. Martin's, 1992); and Deirdre Collings (ed.), *Peace for Lebanon? From War to Reconstruction* (Boulder: Lynne Rienner, 1994).

2. Royal Canadian Mounted Police, *National Drug Intelligence Estimates* (Ottawa: Supply and Services, Canada, 1990), p. 27.

3. Andre McNicoll, *Drug Trafficking: A North-South Perspective* (Ottawa: North-South Institute, 1983), p. 60.

4. Quoted in International Peace Research Association, *Peacebuilding and Development in Lebanon* [Final Conference Report] (Paris: IPRI/UNESCO, 1990), p. 48.

5. The following section was written by Mary B. Anderson, drawing on analysis originally done by Greg Hansen as he wrote the case study but also incorporating lessons learned from many cases over the years of the Local Capacities for Peace Project.

6. Greg Hansen, unpublished case study written for Local Capacities for Peace Project, p. 36.

7. Ibid., p. 39.

8. Ibid., p. 34.

9. This section is from ibid., p. 32.

Chapter 9

Lena Sallin acknowledged the help of the staff of the Cooperation-Dissemination Division and the Africa Operations Sector of the ICRC in Geneva and the ICRC field staff and members of the working group in Burundi, as well as members of the theater group, students, journalists, representatives of human rights organizations, and representatives of UNHCR and UNICEF whom she interviewed. She especially acknowledged the contributions of Ould Abdullah, the UN Special Envoy to Burundi.

1. This section is based on Zdenek Cervenka and Colin Legum, *Can National Dialogue Break the Power of Terror in Burundi?* (Uppsala: Scandinavian Institute of African Studies, 1994); *Utrikespolitiska institutets småskrifter, Rwanda, Burundi* (Stockholm: Scandinavian Institute of African Studies, 1991); and D. Philippin, *The Humanitarian Crisis in the Great Lakes Region* (Geneva: ICRC, February 1995).

2. Conflicts covered by the 1949 Geneva Conventions and the additional protocols of 1977.

3. Conflicts *not* covered by the Geneva Conventions or the additional protocols but in which the ICRC has the power to offer its services because of its right to initiative.

4. In situations of armed conflict and in internal disturbances and tension, the ICRC occupies a unique position among international aid agencies, in part because of its responsibility for overseeing the development of International Humanitarian Law (IHL) and in part because of the rights and obligations invested in it by the Geneva Conventions of 1949. The main instruments of IHL are the four Geneva Conventions of 1949, the two additional protocols of 1977, and the Hague regulations of 1868. Article 3, common to all four Geneva Conventions, expresses the essence of IHL and states the minimal rules to be respected at all times and in all places, independent of the legal status of the conflict.

Within the ICRC, the word *dissemination* refers specifically to activities aimed at making known the contents of IHL, in particular the fundamental humanitarian principles contained therein.

Apart from the contents of IHL, ICRC dissemination activities are also based on the fundamental humanitarian values contained in human rights law and on the seven fundamental principles of the Red Cross movement.

5. This section is adapted from R. Baeriswyl, *La diffusion du droit international humanitaire (DIH): Une contribution du CICR à la prévention et à la limitation des souffrances engendrées par les conflits armés et les situations de violence interne* (Geneva: ICRC, March 22, 1995).

6. This section is based on interviews with ICRC delegates as well as written reports, on interviews with a third of the members of the working group, and on interviews with people involved in the program in Geneva and Burundi.

7. Based on Yolande Diallo, *Traditions africaines et droit humanitaire II* (Geneva: ICRC, 1978), and on interviews carried out in Burundi.

Chapter 10

When he wrote the case, Joe Bock acknowledged the support of the Kellogg National Fellowship Program of the W. K. Kellogg Foundation. Also, special appreciation was given to Fr. Cedric Prakash, director of Saint Xavier's Social Service Society, for his candor, insight, and support.

1. Figures in this section are taken largely from *Urban Environmental Maps for Bombay, Delhi, Ahmedabad, Vadodara* (New Delhi: National Institute of Urban Affairs, February 1994).

2. For helpful background on India's political history, especially as it relates to social integration, see Rakha Saxena, *Indian Politics in Transition: From Dominance to Chaos* (New Delhi: Deep and Deep, 1994), esp. pp. 1–66.

3. The BJP does not reflect the political sentiments of all Hindus. For a succinct explanation of the rise to influence (up to that time) of the BJP, see "The Hindu Upsurge: The Road to Ayodhya," *Economist* (February 6, 1993), pp. 21–23.

4. These explanations are drawn largely from Pravin J. Patel, "Communal Riots in Contemporary India: Towards a Sociological Explanation," in Upendra Baxi and Bhikha Parekh (eds.), *Crisis and Change in Contemporary India* (New Delhi: Sage, 1995), pp. 370–399.

5. Ibid., p. 375.

Chapter 11

When he wrote the case, Stephen Jackson acknowledged the following people for "their generous assistance during my several periods spent in Gedo": Nura Abdi Buled, Naiall Toibin, Joe Feeney, Eamon Meehan, Kathleen Fahey, Liz Higgins, Steven Muninzwa, Abdullahi Ismail Abdullahi "jurat," Vance McGlinchy, Idris Naji, the elders of Bulla Hawa, Tula Bawaaqo, Foolo, and the teachers at the village school in Gawido. He also thanked Isabelle Lomers, Andy Storey, and Laura Frost.

1. Pronounced "Troh-Care-Uh," the name is the Irish word for *compassion*.

2. One useful introduction to the history of this crisis is David Laitin and Said Samatar, *Somalia: Nation in Search of a State* (Boulder: Westview, 1987).

3. The terms *clan* and *tribe* have different meanings for different people. We use them here as suggestive terms rather than definitive classifications.

4. "Population-Based Mortality Assessment—Baidoa and Afgoi, Somalia, 1992," Centers for Disease Control, *Morbidity and Mortality Weekly Report* 41, no. 49 (December 11, 1992).

5. Paolo Freire, *Pedagogy of the Oppressed* (New York: Continuum, [1970] 1993).

6. Although the author was told many times that other agencies followed a "no-guns" strategy, he was unable to obtain specific information about who, where, and when.

7. This term is the English one commonly used by Somalis to describe the Islamic revivalist movements that were trying to extend their influence in southern Somalia at the time the case was written.

8. As the case study was completed, another security incident caused a second suspension of Trocaire's program. This incident involved the stabbing of an expatriate staff member in another town. The elders there assured Trocaire that this was purely a personal vendetta carried out by only one person. Although details are not available about how the crisis was resolved, Trocaire did resume operations soon thereafter.

Chapter 12

1. The Multi-Donor Evaluation of Assistance in Rwanda, led by the Danish Foreign Ministry, in particular made this point.

Bibliographic Essay

Many individuals and institutions have published useful articles, monographs, and books on international assistance and war. I have been challenged by and have learned a great deal from many of them. I cite only a few here, knowing that I leave out even more of equal value and insight. It seems worthwhile to mention a few both to acknowledge their importance to me personally and to provide an initial entrée for readers who do not yet know the field and would like to pursue it in more depth.

The Humanitarianism and War Project, codirected by Thomas Weiss and Larry Minear, located at the Watson Institute at Brown University, has published numerous books and monographs of use to both practitioners and theorists. I cannot include the full list here. One of particular interest historically because it was among the first works to open up a number of critical issues encountered by humanitarians working in war settings is *Humanitarianism Across Borders: Sustaining Civilians in Times of War* (ed. Thomas G. Weiss and Larry Minear, Lynne Rienner, 1993).

The War-Torn Societies Project of the United Nations Research Institute for Social Development (UNRISD) in Geneva publishes regular reports on postconflict situations and has initiated active on-the-ground programs to assist societies as they emerge from war. One that will lead readers to the wider literature is *Conflict, Postwar Rebuilding, and the Economy: A Critical Review of the Literature* by Gilles Carbonnier (Geneva: UNRISD, War-Torn Societies Project, 1998).

Conciliation Resources: An International Service for Conflict Prevention and Resolution in London is also a source of thoughtful reflection. "Supporting Local Capacities for Handling Violent Conflict: A Role for International NGOs?" by Andy Carl, codirector of the center, is an example; it highlights some of the "key issues for INGOs [international nongovernmental organizations] supporting local peacemaking capacities." Conciliation Resources also publishes "An International Review of Peace Initiatives" titled *Accord*; each issue deals with a specific area of conflict. These publications provide detailed narratives and analyses of specific war and peace processes written by different scholars and practitioners.

The Center for Concern in Washington, D.C., and its director, John Prendergast, have provided several of the best analyses of the effects of aid on conflict, especially in the Horn of Africa. See, for example, John Prendergast, *Front-*

155

line Diplomacy: Humanitarian Aid and Conflict in Africa (Lynne Rienner, 1996), which documents the ways aid has reinforced conflict in that region and articulates principles and "commandments" that point the way to giving aid that does not sustain conflict.

The U.S. Institute of Peace, Washington, D.C., regularly supports consultations and conferences that further collective learning and also publishes monographs by its staff and others that add to the aid community's understanding. *Managing Global Chaos: Sources of and Responses to International Conflict* (ed. Chester A. Crocker and Fen Osler Hampson with Pamela Aall, Washington, D.C., United States Institute of Peace Press, 1996) provides a broad introduction to a range of issues that affect current tendencies toward war, including reflections on the roles of international mediation, peacekeeping, humanitarianism, and diplomacy.

The Life and Peace Institute in Uppsala, Sweden, regularly publishes the *Horn of Africa Bulletin,* which frequently deals directly with the relationship between aid and conflict. The Carnegie Commission on Preventing Deadly Conflict of the Carnegie Corporation of New York produced several useful documents during its deliberations, culminating in the final report entitled *Preventing Deadly Conflict* (Carnegie Corporation of New York, 1997).

Hugo Slim, who directs the Complex Emergencies Programme of the Centre for Development and Emergency Planning at Oxford Brookes University in Oxford, England, writes some of the freshest—and to me most helpful—articles that take the challenges of doing better work seriously and position them in the context of history, culture, and international humanitarianism. Two challenging examples are "The Stretcher and the Drum: Civil-Military Relations in Peace Support Operations" (paper presented at the conference "Beyond the Emergency: Development with United Nations Peace Missions," Pretoria, South Africa, March 1996) and "Planning Between Danger and Opportunity: NGO Situation Analysis in Conflict Related Emergencies" (published in the *Journal of Humanitarian Assistance,* May 1996).

Finally, the recently issued *Prevention and Management of Violence Conflicts: An International Directory* (Utrecht: European Platform for Conflict Prevention and Transformation, 1998) includes a listing of almost 500 organizations involved in international work in conflict settings and a series of useful introductory articles.

Index

Afghanistan, 10, 19, 26, 27, 28, 61
Aid agency relationships, 56
Aid distribution: for intergroup
    projects, 34, 35, 39, 47–49, 89; as
    legitimizing conflict, 39, 50–53, 56;
    local decisionmaking in, 47–49,
    87–88, 135, 139; targeting
    subgroups for, 46–49
Aid publicity, 59
Aid resources, 37–39, 69(fig); imported, 42–45, 52; and local
    economy, 39, 42–45, 140;
    protection of, 38, 39–42, 55–56; as
    substitution for local resources,
    49–50
Aid theft. *See* Aid resources,
    protection of
Aid workers, 117, 146; in analysis of
    aid impact, 72–73; and assessment
    of individual conflicts, 20–22,
    33–35; attitudes of, 19–20, 59,
    60–62; lifestyles of, 56–58, 62–63;
    locally hired, 43–45, 47, 58, 87,
    128, 136, 139, 141; postconflict
    planning of, 14, 19, 47; protection
    of, 42, 55–56, 63–66, 136, 138, 141,
    154n6), 154n8
Armed protection. *See* Security

Barre, Mohamed Siad, 132, 133
Bosnia, 26, 29, 30, 48
Burundi, 30, 105–107,109–118;
    conflict in, 105–107; declaration of

humanitarian behavior in,
    109–113, 117; dissemination of
    declaration in, 113–116, 117
Buyoya, Pierre, 106

CAP. *See* Community Awareness
    Program
Catholic Relief Services (CRS), 122,
    134
Children, 19, 28, 29, 30; in India, 122,
    124, 125; in Lebanon, 30, 94, 96–98
Citizens' forums, 26
Civilian society; nonwar actions in,
    24–29. *See also* Connectors
Civilian welfare; local responsibility
    for, 52–53
Civil wars, civilian-based, 11–13;
    attitudinal change during, 20–22
Clans: in Somalia, 27, 132, 133, 138,
    141, 154n3
Codes of conduct, 12–13; in Burundi,
    110–112
Cold War, 9, 132
Colombia, 14
Communications systems, 25, 26. *See
    also* Media
Communists, 82
Community Awareness Program
    (CAP) (Somalia), 135–136, 141
Conflicts, 7; assessing individual,
    20–22, 33–35; political solutions to,
    145–147. *See also* Peace, capacities
    for; War, capacities for

157

About the Book

Echoing the words of the Hippocratic oath, the author of *Do No Harm* challenges aid agency staff members to take responsibility for the ways their assistance affects conflicts.

Anderson cites the experiences of many aid providers in war-torn societies to show that international assistance—even when it is effective in saving lives, alleviating suffering, and furthering sustainable development—too often reinforces divisions among contending groups. But, more important, she offers hopeful evidence of creative programs that point the way to new approaches to aid. Calling for a redesign of assistance programs so they do no harm while doing their intended good, Anderson argues further that many opportunities exist for aid workers to support the processes by which societies disengage from war.

Mary B. Anderson, a development economist, is president of the Collaborative for Development Action. She is coauthor of *Rising from the Ashes: Development Strategies in Times of Disaster.*